# Silko, Morrison, and Roth

# Studies on Themes and Motifs in Literature

Horst S. Daemmrich
*General Editor*

Vol. 37

PETER LANG
New York • Washington, D.C./Baltimore • Boston
Bern • Frankfurt am Main • Berlin • Vienna • Paris

Naomi R. Rand

# Silko, Morrison, and Roth

## Studies in Survival

PETER LANG
New York • Washington, D.C./Baltimore • Boston
Bern • Frankfurt am Main • Berlin • Vienna • Paris

**Library of Congress Cataloging-in-Publication Data**
Rand, Naomi R.
Silko, Morrison, and Roth: studies in survival / Naomi R. Rand.
p. cm. — (Studies on themes and motifs in literature; vol. 37)
Includes bibliographical references.
1. American fiction—20th century—History and criticism. 2. Survival in literature.
3. Silko, Leslie, 1948– —Criticism and interpretation. 4. Morrison, Toni—
Criticism and interpretation. 5. Women and literature—United States—History—
20th century. 6. Roth, Philip—Criticism and interpretation. I. Title. II. Series:
Studies on themes and motifs in literature; vol. 37.
PS374.S85R36   813'.5409353—dc21   97-32320
ISBN 0-8204-3949-5
ISSN 1056-3970


**Die Deutsche Bibliothek-CIP-Einheitsaufnahme**
Rand, Naomi R.:
Silko, Morrison, and Roth: studies in survival / Naomi R. Rand.
–New York; Washington, D.C./Baltimore; Boston; Bern;
Frankfurt am Main; Berlin; Vienna; Paris: Lang.
(Studies on themes and motifs in literature; Vol. 37)
ISBN 0-8204-3949-5


The paper in this book meets the guidelines for permanence and durability
of the Committee on Production Guidelines for Book Longevity
of the Council of Library Resources.

© 1999 Peter Lang Publishing, Inc., New York

All rights reserved.
Reprint or reproduction, even partially, in all forms such as microfilm,
xerography, microfiche, microcard, and offset strictly prohibited.

Printed in the United States of America

# Acknowledgments

Articles based on the material in this book appear in *Melus*, *North Dakota Review*, and *Mosaic*.

# Table of Contents

| | |
|---|---:|
| Introduction | 1 |
| Chapter One: Tales of Power | 17 |
| Chapter Two: *Storyteller*; *The Bluest Eye*; and *Goodbye, Columbus*: Promontories of Power | 27 |
| Chapter Three: Lonely Hearts Beat as One: The Importance of Family | 65 |
| Chapter Four: The Ghost: A Link Between Two Worlds | 93 |
| Chapter Five: Afterward | 109 |
| Bibliography | 113 |

# Introduction

Survivors of a disaster write personal narratives for complex psychological reasons. Sometimes they are attempting to thwart further injustice, sometimes they are bearing witness as a way of reordering a world gone mad. Whatever the reason behind the desire to testify, it is obvious that survivors pay a lifelong price for their own miraculous escape from personal obliteration.

Leslie Marmon Silko, Philip Roth, and Toni Morrison are writers from different ethnic backgrounds. These three would seem to have little in common, yet each one comes from a marginalized ethnic background. I would argue that these writers choose to adopt the survivor's stance. They testify to a history, be it Native American, Jewish American or African American, that they see as a history of victimization. Yet while they offer up that argument, they also grapple with the knowledge of their own singular escape and the guilt it entails.

A close examination of six texts reveals an interesting and telling parallel; these writers create protagonists who exhibit many of the key traits noted by those who have studied the survivor's psyche.

In *Storyteller, Goodbye, Columbus,* and *The Bluest Eye*, Silko, Roth, and Morrison create narrators who avail themselves of a pseudo-scientific pose. These "I" narrators distance themselves from the stories they relate. As a "scientist," each becomes someone who is able to dissect and examine a treacherous world from a place of physical if not emotional safety.

These scientific narrators are survivors who have always existed at a remove from victims. This is the paradigm Bruno Bettelheim argued for in "Individual and Mass Behavior in Extreme Situations,"[1] which detailed Bettelheim's own experience as an inmate in two German concentration camps, Dachau and Buchenwald. Bettelheim claimed that the article explored "certain aspects of the far-reaching psychological impact the camps had directly on their inmates, and indirectly on the population under Nazi domination" (48). [2]

A heroic individualist, Bettelheim's survivor was capable of living both inside and outside the narrative. In this case, Bettelheim himself claimed a degree of nobility; he was writing the article so that the world would know the horrors of Nazism. However, two current biographies note that he also took advantage of this extreme situation to reconstruct his persona. Though Bettelheim entered the camps a member of the merchant class, he left as a self-described psychologist.[3]

This desire to heroicize and elevate the captive self is mirrored in the work of Silko, Roth, and Morrison.[4] Bettelheim exaggerated his own experience in order to give himself credibility.[5] What might be seen as a personal failing in the normal world becomes an integral part of his "survivor's" personality. Bettelheim proposes this new self as personal savior. Looking at it another way, you could say that Bettelheim must rationalize his own escape and so he devises rational explanations for it after the fact. But think of Art Spiegelman's father in *Maus:* "in some ways he's just like the racist caricature of the miserly old Jew" (131). His father was always like this, hoarding and pinching pennies. Yet this abrasive cheapness could have helped him during the worst days of the Holocaust. It is hard to say what comes first, but traits that were perhaps originally part of a person's psyche are deepened in unpredictable ways by an "extreme" experience.

Despite copious literature disputing his psychological analysis of inmate behavior, Bettelheim argued that his view was the most psychologically correct. He presented himself as an authority on the Holocaust. "As a victim of the camps he was 'an irreproachable witness, a steady voice in a chorus of interpreters,' " (Pollak 383). For years, his harsh assessment of the behavior of long-term inmates caused controversy.[6] However, a different reading of Bettelheim's slim analysis provides him with an escape and an emotional freedom from internment. He is the scientist, busy with his study, and this ability to sever himself from the rest becomes his route to salvation.

Primo Levi separated those in the camps into two distinct groups, the drowned and the saved. And anyone who has been instructed in the basics of water safety understands that the first thing you must do with drowners is disable them. They cling instinctively to anyone who tries to rescue them, often dragging the rescuer below the surface. Bettelheim saw those interned with him as drowners. He believed that they would destroy him. He distanced himself emotionally, creating a psychology of "them" versus "me." His ability to garner the support of social scientists, scholars, and intellectuals makes his escape even more compelling.

Bettelheim asks, "'How can I protect myself against becoming as they are?'" (52).[7] His answer is the study: "By occupying myself during my spare time with interesting problems, by talking with my fellow prisoners with a particular purpose in mind, by pondering my findings for the hours without end during which I was forced to perform exhausting labor which did not ask for any mental concentration, I succeeded in killing the time in a way which seemed constructive" (52).[8]

Interned under inhuman conditions, Bettelheim depended on what was most canny in him. He used his own experience as a subject of unfinished analysis to reconstruct himself as a social scientist.[9] Others chose ways to integrate their earlier self. Levi wrote, "Culture was useful. . . . Not always, at times perhaps by subterranean and unforeseen paths, but it served me well and perhaps it saved me (*Drowned* 139). And Langer offers this artist's testimony: "My commitment to drawing came out of a deep instinct of self-preservation and undoubtedly helped me to deny the unimaginable horrors of that time. By taking the role of an 'observer' I could at least for a few moments detach myself from what was going on in Auschwitz" (Langer, Introduction).

Bettelheim was both observer and psychological bellwether. Using a third-person narrator to describe his version of life in a madhouse, he is the dispassionate observer. Others metamorphose and suddenly appear "to be pathological liars, to be unable to restrain their emotional outbursts" (52). Others are unable "to make objective evaluations" (52). And Bettelheim had other ways of promoting himself as a normal, rational being. He waited for nearly three years before deciding to submit his paper for publication because "his anger about the treatment he had received might endanger his objectivity" (54). By offering this rationalization for his actions, Bettehleim further promoted the concept of a normal evaluative procedure operating under the most abnormal conditions.[10]

Bettelheim offers an apparently rational explanation for his behavior, yet in almost in the next breath he discards the idea of a dispassionate discussion. This article was written as a weapon, and Bettelheim's hope is that public opinion will be aroused. His article will be ammunition in a war against the Gestapo (54). He is not the emotionally distanced narrator he initially pretends to be. Indeed, this study has a baldly political purpose. His findings are intended to arouse and inflame.

Survivors talk of their sense of obligation, their need to testify. "We must not become beasts; that even in this place one can survive, and therefore one must want to survive, to tell the story, to bear witness" (Levi, *Survival in Auschwitz* 36). However, Bettelheim is a peculiar example. His sense of obligation to his comrades vies with his keen desire for self-preservation.

Lawrence Langer theorizes that extreme events eradicate the familiar. Survivors end up divorced from our own socially accepted sense of historical time. Holocaust survivors relive their experiences as they relate them; the past is so harsh that it obliterates all that has come after. Bettelheim's life *in extremis* submerged the self he had known before; his experience in the camps remade him. In his case the internal became the external; his remade personality, his new position as an authority on the survivor's experience, was a way of living, in that most immediate of moments forever.

Bettelheim acknowledged the difficulty of the task he set for himself:

> The difficulty of analyzing mass behavior when the investigator is part of the group being analyzed should also be apparent. Moreover, the personal difficulty of observing and reporting objectively on situations which arouse the strongest emotions when experienced ought to be mentioned. The writer is aware of these limitations on his objectivity and only hopes that he has succeeded in overcoming some of them (55).

Despite this initial inclusion of self, Bettelheim immediately separated himself from the group. His personal anecdotes detailed his own response to incarceration, but they quickly led to generalizations about other inmates' behavior. If one reads his study as a narrative of personal survival rather than an accurate rendering of camp life, the progression is obvious. Incarceration gives way to disbelief; then, quickly, self-preservation becomes of the order of the day. Bettelheim's principal task is to quantify the differences between himself the survivor and the mass of victims who surround him.[11]

In Terrence Des Pres's *The Survivor,* a different archetype is created. Des Pres's survivor is heroic, generous when generosity can no longer be imagined. Des Pres imagines the group of inmates working in solidarity, spinning gold from flax. His view of humanity is supremely Lockeian, and completely opposite to Bettelheim's. It is no surprise that when Des Pres's book was published, Bettelheim launched a vicious assault. He blames Des Pres for making "survivors appear unusual, most superior persons because of their experiences in the extermination camps" (95). However, this is an accurate assessment of his own work. Bettelheim believes that Des Pres's book "draws our attention away from the millions who were murdered. . . . It makes heroes out of these chance survivors" (95). But his own description of camp life depended on his own heroicization. In turn, Des Pres castigated Bettelheim for his individualism stance. Noting the limits of psychoanalytic interpretation, Des Pres pointed out that "Bettelheim's idea of heroism dovetails with the view of man as victim" (163). Des Pres critiqued Bettelheim's superior perch, noting that his attitude "is evident not only in the sense of isolation and superiority which attends references to himself, but also in an animus toward other prisoners generally" (159).

Bettelheim's discussion covered public and private behavior. The public behavior described in his article is the most deeply distressing to readers like Des Pres. Bettelheim drew a rigid line between the behaviors of "older" and "newer" prisoners, defining older prisoners as those who have been incarcerated for at least three years. It would seem reasonable to expect a well-argued explanation for this dividing line, but none is ever provided. However, Bettelheim spent only ten months in the camps.[12] According to him, older prisoners were the ones who "made their peace with the values of the SS" and "firmly believed that the rules set down by the SS were desirable standards of human behavior, at least within the camp situation" (81). Older prisoners were therefore sometimes

> instrumental in getting rid of the "unfit.". . . This was one of many situations in which old prisoners would demonstrate toughness, having molded their treatment of these "unfit" prisoners to the example set by the SS. Self-protection required elimination of the "unfit" prisoners, but the way in which they were sometimes tortured for days by the old prisoners and slowly killed was taken over from the gestapo (79).

Lawrence Langer argues that "Bettelheim's early charge that the least successful camp inmates regressed to passive and childlike behavior instead of choosing defiant and assertive postures. . . . [shaped] habits of mind that are difficult to dislodge" (181). Indeed,

Bettelheim's assertions have created an image of inmates' behavior that must be reckoned with, either through argument or through some sort of reasoned acceptance. But Langer has misread the text.[13] Bettelheim does not claim that it is the weaker inmates who cling to these childlike behaviors. He makes no judgment about weakness; rather, he uses length of internment as the cutoff. Bettelheim offers evidence of infantilization, that renders a judgment. Yet he purports to make no judgment at all. I would argue that he does this to further illustrate his own superiority. He, the new prisoner, could never act like these beaten-down, morally helpless, hopeless victims.

The idea of any individual's control over personal destiny in an arena so overwhelmingly brutal seems little more than ridiculous. Yet, though Bettelheim admits this, noting that "survival in the camps—this cannot be stressed enough—depended foremost on luck" and adding that "nothing one could do could assure survival," he also swings back to a belief in the power of the personal (*Surviving and Other Essays* 108). Though "chances were at best extremely slim, one could increase them through correctly assessing one's situation and taking advantage of opportunities; in short, through acting independently and with courage, decision and conviction, all of which depended on the measure of autonomy one had managed to retain" (108).

In *Individual and Mass Behavior in Extreme Situations*, Bettelheim constructs his own heroic survival myth. He is the warrior, clinging to self despite the relentless and numbing power of the Nazi hierarchy. Although there are moments of despair when he is worn down, he manages to pursue his quest, in this case his grail-like study. Bettelheim argues that the Nazi state demanded an obliteration of the personal: "the individual as such was either non-existent or of no importance" (49). So his desire to heroicize singularity becomes a double act of rebellion, both self-preserving and subversive. And his rebellion is much safer than physical defiance of authority, since open hostility to the powers that be, however heroic, could end in death. And to further point out the immoral power of such heroics, Bettelheim notes that "if a prisoner tried to protect a group, he might be killed by a guard, but if his action came to the knowledge of the camp administration, then the whole group was always punished more severely than it would have been in the first place" (67). By devaluing heroic acts, Bettelheim elevates his own "private" choice. He juggles a desire for safety with a need to imagine that his safety has not been bought at too terrible a price. And he emerges, like a true hero, unscathed, his psyche unscarred.

Robert Jay Lifton's study of Hiroshima survivors notes how survivors' guilt shapes their lives afterwards.

> Death, especially when inappropriate and premature, is the essence of breakdown and separation. In identifying so strongly with the dead—in forming what we have called the identity of the dead—the survivor seeks both to atone for his participation in that breakdown, and to reconstitute a form of order around that atonement (497).

Lifton offers the phrase "death in life" as a way of defining the survivor's emotional state. Survivors can no longer believe in or depend on the social order that we, in our naivete, take for granted. And why should they? Their experience has tainted everything. Even if they readjust to the world and lead seemingly normal lives, history dogs their memory. They can never fully trust in normality. And guilt is their shadow language.

In Bettelheim's case, guilt was transformative, giving him a superior position. Throughout his life Bettelheim promoted himself as a supreme authority on camp life. This desire for exclusivity informs his critiques of other scholars. He derided Lifton for equating "Auschwitz with Hiroshima or My Lai" (94). But in attacking Lifton for generalizing, he became guilty of the same sort of diminishment. Bettelheim defines My Lai as one of many "isolated homicidal outbreaks of war" (94). Then he equates it with the devastation of Hiroshima, belittling both while elevating the Holocaust experience and going on to position Jews as the only truly innocent victims:

> Equating what the Nazis did with the American bombing of Hiroshima seems on the surface a more appropriate comparison, since in both instances governmental preplanning was responsible for what happened. But it is actually an even more vicious distortion, because it implicitly accepts one of the biggest Nazi lies as truth—namely, that the Jews were an enemy waging aggressive war against Germany. In reality, as is well known, the Jews were Germany's most peaceful and tragically obedient subjects (95).

Bettelheim's argument elevates the experience of Jewish survivors while devaluing the more inclusive humanist viewpoint

Lifton proposes: "after Hiroshima, we can envisage no war-linked chivalry, certainly no glory. Indeed, we can see no relationship—not even a distinction—between victimizer and victim, only the sharing in species annihilation" (Lifton 541). Bettelheim's desire to privilege the Jews above innocent Japanese or Vietnamese civilians (and above the homosexuals, communists, Gypsies, and other victims of Nazi terror) is another piece of his survivor psychology.[14]

Lifton argues that many survivors privilege their own experience.[15] He catalogues this antipathy toward other marginalized groups as a "suspicion of counterfeit nurturance." But this analysis points out the limits of psychoanalytic theory. This label suggests a tidy Freudian package, presenting survivors as emotionally damaged children responding from past parent-child experiences. As examples of this privileging, Lifton points to African-Americans' anger at the white majority. He also singles out third-world countries who are suspicious of aid packages given them by their former colonial masters. The situations he uses for exemplification have their own historical, social, and political records. But Lifton is content to dehistoricize, to depoliticize.

This privileging is not all negative. Members of ethnic groups who elevate their suffering are not just diminishing others; they are also attempting to foster a connection, a social bond. Ethnic clannishness is an active attempt at self-preservation, a way of developing group solidarity.

In *Almanac of the Dead, Portnoy's Complaint,* and *Song of Solomon,* Silko, Roth, and Morrison reject the individualistic pose Bettelheim depends on. In these novels they create protagonists who defy the code of individualism. These heroes and heroines try to redefine community and repair shattered ethnic bonds, yet as they do they exhibit "suspicion of counterfeit nurturance."

Publicly brutal events like the Holocaust or the dropping of the atomic bomb call into question established views of humanity. Moral codes imprinted since childhood are destroyed in seconds. Indeed, the survivors are no longer able to believe in a positive Lockean view of humanity. Their experience forces them into a vision of humanity as principally evil.

Lifton believes that survivors resent the dead because the dead have deprived them of their "own sense of immortality" (494). He bases this on the psychoanalytical premise that a sense of immortality, a belief in the open-ended nature of one's own life, is a prerequisite to real mental health. But these survivors resent the dead for another, less psychoanalytically profound reason. The dead give testimony to the survivor's lost belief in the reconstructive power of human nature. These ghosts remind the survivor of how untrustworthy the human animal is.[16]

Lifton believes that survivors internalize their anger because they only "accept and internalize the world in which (they have) been victimized, including in some degree the motivation and behavior of the victimizer." Their "quest for adaptation and mastery thus involves (them) in a limited but . . . loathsome 'identification with the aggressor.' " Such identification "in turn contributes to (their) guilt and confusion" (498). This would offer an explanation for the behavior Bettelheim notes in older camp inmates. Lifton sees this behavior as progressive rather than regressive, "adaptation and mastery" become a way for the survivor to remake a damaged psyche.

Lifton's survivors have other psychological tools at their disposal. "Psychic numbing" provides a foolproof way of keeping a psyche intact. Numbing is a two-part process. One part entails a shutting down of emotion; the other part is a more complicated stance and involves distancing oneself from the remembered victims. Bettelheim's article illustrates this; his scientific narrator is remarkably detached from the brutality he delineates.

Still, Lifton's psychoanalytical analysis falls short of the mark. For him, anger is a sign of psychic damage, and he believes that the intensity of anger expressed by survivors comes from a survivor's "need to pass judgement on people and forces outside of himself in order to avoid drowning in his own death guilt and symbolic disorder" (531). Yet if one survives the bombing of Hiroshima, the death camps, if one is a victim of constant and consistent racism, anger becomes a righteous weapon. It is not simply derived from "death guilt." Anger is a rational response, not a neurotic psychological construct. When those who have lived under what they believe is a valid social contract see that contract sundered, anger must be first line of defense.

Lifton's and Bettelheim's psychoanalytical approaches depend on a standard for "normality." Thus Bettelheim can claim that this incarceration is beyond the boundaries of known experience even as he falls back on socially accepted psychoanalytical definitions which were used to describe life under nonextreme conditions: "At first he rationalized that these changes in behavior were only surface phenomena, the logical result of his peculiar situation. But soon he realized that the split of his person into one who observed and one to whom things happened could not be called normal, but was typical psychopathological phenomenon"(52). Lawrence Langer and Terence Des Pres present a counterpoint to Bettelheim's and Lifton's psychological arguments. They believe that any real attempt to define "the survivor" must reinvent both the word and the world.

Des Pres's book *The Survivor* offers a challenge to the bleak topology of life in extremity that Bettelheim and Lifton describe. His "subject is survival, the capacity of men and women to live beneath the pressure of protracted crisis, to sustain terrible damage in mind and body and yet be there, sane, alive, still human" (Preface). His survivor clings to humanity. Heroism is dependent on acts that in other circumstances would seem unremarkable. Des Pres argues that we must reimagine our concept of resistance. His survivors resist the weight of oppression through any means at their disposal. In doing so, they experience "a strength beyond hope, as stubborn as the upsurge of spring.... In this state a strange exultation fills the soul, a sense of being equal to the worst. And as long as they live, survivors *are* equal to the worst" (21).

Although Des Pres discusses the arbitrary nature of camp life, he asserts a determinist belief in the power of certain types of human behavior. According to him, Nadezhda Mandelstam "survived to testify, and in that purpose found strength to continue" (34).[17] First survival, then testimony. A desire to testify to the horror becomes incorporated into the psyche. Des Pres believes that "survivors choose life" (24). This determinist belief simply does not jibe with historical fact, for in the death camps chance was often the ultimate arbiter of an inmate's destiny.

Des Pres believes that psychoanalysts misread the survivor's mentality because "the aim of psychiatric treatment is adjustment, acceptance, forgetting—goals which constitute a condition the survivor rejects. The urgency of his need to bear witness puts him in open conflict with the system being imposed to explain away his behavior, and such opposition, from the psychiatric point of view, is further evidence of neurotic reaction" (39). According to Des Pres, assumptions that "the need to bear witness is rooted in neurosis . . . ignore entirely the nature of extreme experience. . . .We cannot know, we have no *way* of knowing, what provokes the survivor's behavior unless we accept at face value the content of his or her story" (44).

Des Pres believes that survivors' primary goal is self-protection, they exert "steady resistance to their obliteration as human beings" (64). One example is an attempt to maintain links with the past self. Primo Levi noted the value of the intellectual discourse that took place in Auschwitz. He believes these discussions provided him with a psychological salvation, making it possible for him "to reestablish a link with the past, saving it from oblivion and reinforcing my identity" (*The Drowned and the Saved* 139). And Bettelheim describes "the *politically educated prisoners*" as being the best equipped for incarceration. In a perverse twist, they "found support for their self-esteem in the fact that the gestapo had singled them out as important enough to take revenge on" (56).

Bettelheim invokes the power of the individual, but Des Pres argues that the individual could not survive without the group working on his or her behalf. Des Pres's politically active prisoners dared to defy those in authority and sacrificed themselves with a certain nameless splendor. "Life was preserved because men and women did not hesitate when moments of hard choice arose. If, as happened at Auschwitz, some members of the resistance got caught, the rest of the organization had to be protected" (130). Des Pres notes that poison was smuggled to the captured and "rather than revealing the names of their comrades, they . . . committed suicide" (Des Pres 130). Bettelheim agrees that "the prisoners, to survive, had to help each other" (286). However, he also notes the guards' vindictive response to any act of courage.

However, there is one way in which Bettelheim's survivor jibes with Des Pres's analysis. Bettelheim believed that camp life "taught us that there is meaning in life, difficult though that meaning may be to fathom—a much deeper meaning than we had thought possible before we became survivors. And our feeling of guilt for having been so lucky as to survive the hell of the concentration camp is a most significant part of this meaning—testimony to a humanity that not even the abomination of the concentration camp can destroy" (314).[18]

It would be well-nigh impossible for most survivors to see themselves as purely heroic using normal criteria. Still, Des Pres is convincing when he tells us that "the hardness of the survivor's choice . . . requires a toughness equal in its way to the forces he or she resists; life goes on by using the methods of the enemy" (129). However, survivors who have used those methods feel no great assurance in their own standards of moral toughness, for the choices are horrific:

> My mother was very weak and began to collapse and fall on her side. So I helped her up and tried to drag her along. . . . I was suffocating from the smoke and I thought if we stayed like this, then both of us would be killed. I thought if I could reach the wider road, I could get some help, so I left my mother there and went off (Lifton 40).

Des Pres is an optimist. He sees the survivor as a kind of totem. This figure should prove to us that "men and women are now strong enough, mature enough, awake enough, to face death without mediation, and therefore embrace life without reserve" (207). Bettelheim believes that Des Pres's phrase "life without reserve" refers to the survivors he describes. But I would argue that he refers, instead, to his audience. Des Pres wants his survivor to offer an object lesson. "Life without reserve" means a life with moral cohesion where the connection and devotion of the group prove that civilization is still a workable construct.

Of these four writers, Lawrence Langer is the only one who believes that extreme experience is totally outside the bounds of what we know. Langer argues for constant confrontation with the reality of the Holocaust. He does not define; he simply challenges all easily reasoned interpretations. He is the theorist who seems to capture the mindset of the survivor most completely. For the survivor is someone in flux, trying on poses, attempting reattachment to a social order he or she is no longer comfortable with, and ultimately inventing new worlds in a dramatic attempt to integrate past and present experience. Ultimately, survivors know that their existence is due to a potent combination; internal strength has meshed with the most powerful and most irrational of weapons, simple luck. This is why, when we attempt to define the survivor's world, we are trying to define the ineffable.

Langer attempts empathy. He imagines himself as "they" are. He believes that the "discourse of consolation" which has surrounded Holocaust studies and the study of survival should be discarded. There can be no consolation, and any attempt to find hope is a lie. For Langer, the Holocaust, that moment of extremity, stands outside of history, always present, always vivid.

Langer positions himself at a remove from Des Pres and he believes that Bettelheim's early view of complicity presented a disturbing precedent which led other writers and theoreticians to blame the victims of the Holocaust. He accuses Lifton of humanistic naivete.[19] Langer, like Des Pres, argues against applying our normal psychological boundaries to the Holocaust. "We will not begin to understand how the Holocaust could have happened until we abandon simplified moral and psychological categories like doubling and conscience and regard the mind of the perpetrators as another landscape in concrete, alive but lacking the vital signs we are accustomed to seeing there" (182).[20] Yet he believes that Des Pres has minimized the individual and in so doing has both romanticized and reimagined the Holocaust in a most unreal way, fortifying "a myth instead of exposing a truth" (183).

For Langer, the extremity of this situation causes it to stand outside of all that is recognizable. The primary lesson this sort of suffering teaches is the fact of the suffering itself. Perhaps only art can move beyond the boundaries of real experience. This is what these writers attempt, imagining a world where survivors can argue with a brutal past and emerge, scarred but capable of continuance. When Nathan Zuckerman bargains with Anne Frank's ghost, he attempts to construct this sort of world. So does Tayo when he makes love with the Ka'atsina spirit. So does Sethe when she submits to the tortures of Beloved.

Bettelheim, Lifton, DesPres, and Langer offer different descriptions of a survivor's psyche. In examining these texts I have turned to each of them as a way of enlarging my analysis. I suppose that, like Lifton, I am eager to universalize. Yet I do not do so out of naivete. Each ethnic group has faced truly unique difficulties. Silko, Morrison, and Roth have vastly different historical and social concerns. Philip Roth's terrain is the world of Jewish guilt engendered by familial pressures and compounded by the Holocaust. Leslie Marmon Silko never lets the reader forget the genocide practiced against the Indians and the daily obliteration of Native American civilizations. Toni Morrison speaks of racism, the historical roots and the ever-present, deadly aftereffects of the slave trade.

For each one of these writers, history is a critical element. In the novels I analyze, heroes and heroines encounter a multitude of trials and tribulations, but the central issue is survival. These narrators are recounting their escape. And these novels all depend on an ever-present danger; the possibility of cultural and physical obliteration. None of these narratives is a true-life story. None tells us about concentration camps, the Gulag or the aftereffects of an atomic blast. And the horror we feel when reading about the fiercest kind of real-life tragedies is not the type of horror we feel when he read fiction. Yet fiction can be composed for the same reason. It can be both explanatory and exculpatory. These writers too feel a need to "tell the story, to bear witness" (Des Pres 36).

**Notes**

[1] Originally published in *Journal of Abnormal and Social Psychology* in 1943, pp. 417-452.

[2] Bettelheim proposed this short piece as a real study of the effects of Nazi internment, this despite his admission that he was basing his analysis on a mass of "observations."

[3] See Sutton and Pollak.

[4] That Bettelheim also travels to America and becomes someone else fits in neatly with our vision of new world versus old world, America as the land of endless opportunity.

[5] See Sutton and see Pollak.

[6] According to Pollak, Terence Des Pres "faulted Bettelheim for the kind of oversimplification and lack of context that marked so much of his Holocaust writing" (376).

[7] Lawrence Langer notes that in the camp setting "most human beings were stripped of the luxury of caring for anyone but one's own" (*Admitting the Holocaust* 45).

[8] These interviews also performed another function: they offered Bettelheim a new personality, constructed in the camps, that he then depended on afterwards. For many, destruction of their past life is a curse; for Bettelheim, it appears to be a blessing. See Pollak.

[9] He also used bribery to get special favors, a side of his incarceration that he hid. Bettelheim was obsessed with his image.

[10] Of course this concept is the underpinning of any psychoanalytical framework. And any attempt to argue with normal versus abnormal contexts would undermine his new version of self.

¹¹Bettelheim notes that prisoners fall into various categories: politically educated prisoners, nonpolitical middle-class prisoners, and upper-class prisoners. He never explains which category he fall into, but he does hint at his own political affiliation. This has never been substantiated. Sutton is more generous in her analysis.

¹²Exaggerated into a year in his foreword.

¹³Or perhaps he refers to the socially accepted response to this text.

¹⁴Bettelheim eulogizes the Jewish dead, calling them the only innocent victims. Yet even as he elevates these victims, he manages to castigate them. His harsh assessment of the Frank family's complicity in their own extermination is a prime example.

¹⁵ Lifton uses a performance by Amira Baraka as an example. He notes that Baraka is dismissive of Jewish suffering, focusing instead on the African American condition. Baraka (then Leroi Jones) "speaks of his dramatic group as 'a theater of victims' . . . and dismisses two white civil rights workers murdered in the South as mere 'artifacts'" (512-513). Lifton believes that Baraka is "telling us that *anything* offered by the hated white giver, even his life, must be counterfeit" (513). Lifton goes on to describe the "sense of rivalry" between groups who believe themselves victims: "the sense of victim consciousness has become so extreme that the 'survivor' of racial abuse takes on a hardened psychic stance in which he no longer is aware of human beings, only victims and victimizers" (513). This perfectly describes Bettelheim's clannish response.

¹⁶In remembering the dead, survivors also relive their own selfish thoughts and actions. One Hiroshima survivor describes how his wife died and the accompanying daily guilt. "It was strange but when she died, I did not feel extremely sad. . . . Of course, I did not have enough knowledge at the time, but since then I have said to myself constantly: I wish I could have given her more care and attention" (Lifton 41).

¹⁷Mandelstam is the wife of the famous Russian poet, a victim of Stalin's purges.

[18] There is one area, in particular, where Des Pres contradicts Bettelheim most effectively. Des Pres has a completely different explanation for inmate imitation and adoption of Nazi styles and attitudes. Instead of seeing this "mimicry" of the Nazi jailer as a sign of internal psychic degeneration, Des Pres (using a great deal of narrative support) makes a claim for mimicry as a form of resistance. He writes that "imitation of SS behavior was a regular feature of life in the camps, and the large numbers of prisoners benefited because positions of power were secretly used in ways which assisted the general struggle for life" (118). Bettelheim refuses to imagine useful purposes other than self-preservation. His desire to psychoanalyze, this need to disguise the self, is of course reflexive. By denoting these prisoners as psychologically damaged, he inflates his own position as therapist and observer.

[19] Langer finds fault with Lifton's study of Nazi doctors. He claims that it is another example of historians who ignore the testimony of the victims while "turning with fascination to the oral testimony of the perpetrators" (182).

[20] Still, he believes that Des Pres provides us with a revisionist view of the survivor and he finds Des Pres's reconstruction of a narrative hero-heroine the weakest part of his argument.

# Chapter One:
# Tales of Power

The six fictional survival narratives presented here examine the impossibility of cultural integration. Indeed, they debunk the myth of the melting pot. Silko, Roth, and Morrison offer critical views of their protagonists' lives, lives that are informed by ethnic history and can only be sustained by a precarious balancing act. The heroes and heroines live in a gap between two worlds: the world of the saved and the world of the drowned.

These culturally marginalized protagonists all attempt assimilation and fail. Their failure comes because of historical barriers based on long-held racist and anti-Semitic beliefs. In creating these protagonists, the writers expose their own complicated connection to their ethnicity.

Philip Roth has constantly written about the pull of his old-world Jewish roots. In *Portnoy's Complaint* Alex speaks of his desire for the past, for the things he has ostensibly rejected. His tone is faintly satirical, but there is a tangible longing in his descriptions: "those men! I want to grow up to *be* one of those men! To be going home to Sunday dinner at one o'clock, sweat socks pungent from twenty-one innings of softball, underwear athletically gamy" (245). Portnoy's vision of this paradise is tongue-in-cheek. We know he is "Assistant Commissioner of Human Opportunity" and doesn't really want to be "a robust Jewish man now gloriously pooped—yes, home I head for resuscitation . . . and to whom? To *my* wife and *my* children, to a family of my own, and right there in the Weequahic section" (245). Portnoy has no intention of returning to New Jersey (his ranting to the psychiatrist details his escape from there). He has moved across the Hudson and through a host of women's bodies. Yet Portnoy cannot escape a deep-seated sense of loss. The description of those "Jewish men" is only one example of his faintly suppressed desire for a return to communal Jewish society.

Portnoy's old-world life has been shattered because he has bought into new-world values, the tantalizing promises offered by this bountiful, all-too-feminine America. Portnoy cannot deny the importance of his past. This is why he desperately attempts to find a way of melding the old world and the new.[1]

Silko is also obsessed with the old world, in her case a world where tribal identity gave Native Americans social and political power. Silko reinvents this mythic world. According to Silko, the Laguna Pueblo and other Native American tribal communities exist on two separate planes. There is the temporal plane. This is the place where Indians coexist with an oppressive white majority. Then there is a time-line stretching back tens of thousands of years. This Indian past is so ancient that it supersedes European claims, upending European dominance. Silko uses this historical precedence to debunk Europeans' notion of themselves as the most highly civilized peoples.

In Silko's version of a Native American creation myth, Europeans are created by Gunadeeyahs, or Indian sorcerers. The whites are automatically disempowered, since they are a malevolent invention of the Indians. "Now the old story came back to Sterling as he walked along. The appearance of the Europeans had been no accident; the Gunadeeyahs had called for their white brethren to join them" (*The Almanac of the Dead* 760).

In *Ceremony* Silko creates a protagonist who is born into two worlds. As a half-breed he is ostracized by both whites and Indians. At the end of this novel, Tayo chooses a "voluntary"[2] Indian identity, discarding his link to whiteness. This choice gives him a way of coming to terms with his own dead. In addition, the rejection of whiteness is Silko's way of taking revenge against the brutal white world.[3]

For much of the novel, Tayo hangs between his two worlds. He has difficulty holding onto his sanity. Ultimately, he is able to repair himself emotionally through a sexual interaction with a spiritual healer, a ghost who is also made flesh. Indians understand the healing arts, while the white world demands physical and emotional sacrifices. Rocky, Tayo's cousin, dies fighting a white war. And he is doomed because he has ingested the white man's lies. "He was an A-student and all-state in football and track. He had to win; he said he was always going to win. So he listened to his teachers, and he listened to the coach. They were proud of him. They told him, 'Nothing can stop you now except one thing: don't let the people at home hold you back' " (51).

*Storyteller* depends on tension between Silko, with her scientific (or in this case, anthropological) detachment, and the text. In this book, Silko mixes poetry, memoir, fiction, and myth. The different writing styles reflect her ambivalent attitude. Silko has trouble positioning the narrative "I." Her stories illustrate the impact of white incursions into tribal society. Yet she positions herself outside and above the fray, ensuring herself a place of safety.

*Almanac of the Dead* offers another type of survival strategy. This novel proposes a futuristic world where the oppressors will finally be overrun by armed insurrectionists.[4] In this new mythology, those who are prepared to fight against tyranny (and who understand the call of the mystical snake) will be saved.[5]

Silko describes an upside/down world. She confines white evil inside Indian sorcery and establishes a reverse reservation system. This time the Indians control the white man's future.[6] And she demands compensation. In *Almanac of the Dead* she invents a world where a Native American led revolution will succeed and Indians will retake the land. However, in this, her most ambitious novel, Silko also creates a world gone mad. In this world whites are insanely abusive. Silko ends up imitating the oppressor, using a narrative discourse in her fictional work that depends on racial stereotypes and ultimately, a distressing homophobia.[7] Indeed she seems to imitate and coopt the oppressor's tactics.[8]

Both Philip Roth and Leslie Marmon Silko create protagonists who deal aggressively with their marginalization. In Silko's case, this means actual physical warfare. Roth chooses a different sort of weapon. He has faith in verbal evisceration.

In *Goodbye, Columbus* Neil castigates Brenda for having changed her Jewish nose. And in his book-long complaint, Portnoy castigates the same WASPs he lusts after. "Why didn't I marry the girl? Well, there was her cutesy-wootsy boarding school argot, for one. Couldn't bear it. 'Barf' for vomit, 'ticked off' for angry, 'a howl' for funny. . . . Then my argot caused her some pain too. The first time I said fuck in her presence . . . such a look of agony passed over The Pilgrim's face, you would have thought I had just branded four letters on her flesh. Why, she asked so plaintively once we were alone, why *had* I to be so 'unattractive' " (233). Roth's protagonists use their verbal agility as a call to arms.

Morrison promotes a different kind of revolutionary stance. Although she actively derides whiteness, her novels ignore the particulars of the white world. Morrison's protagonists live and breathe inside a separate world, an African-American community where whites remain uncharacterized and marginalized. Morrison's self-enclosed black communities bear a resemblance to Brenda Patimkin's world. Members of these communities, like Brenda, are caught up in a fantasy; they want to merge with the oppressor. This sort of flattering imitation is clearly self-destructive.

In *Sula* a community destroys itself through this sort of central misunderstanding. The African-American citizens of the Bottom "come out and play in the sunshine—as though the sunshine would last, as though there really was hope. The same hope that kept them picking beans for other farmers; kept them from finally leaving as they talked of doing; kept them knee-deep in other people's dirt; kept them excited about other people's wars; kept them solicitous of white people's children; kept them convinced that some magic 'government' was going to lift them up, out and away from that dirt, those beans, those wars" (160). The townspeople go down to investigate and destroy a mine shaft. They are lost in the vision that possesses them, a vision that Morrison returns to often in her work. They are obsessed with the wrong kind of values, those deeded to them by the dominant white culture. They cannot recognize the most vital pieces of an African-American self. This is why "a lot of them died" in that mine shaft, buried alive because of their misconceived hope (162).

Bettelheim and Des Pres have argued that in the death camps, imitation meant survival. But Morrison disagrees. In these novels any imitation of the white world, indeed any belief in white authority, is devestatingly destructive. Silko's work castigates whites and elevates the Indian. Roth's writing focuses on a duel with a white or Gentile world that tempts and tortures his heroes. And Morrison attempts to create a black-owned world where whites will someday be superfluous.

According to Primo Levi, there is no way to "specify why I, rather than thousands of others, managed to survive the test" (*Survival in Auschwitz* 111). Ultimately, survival is arbitrary. Yet there are ways bettering the odds. In *Goodbye, Columbus*, Roth chooses the simplest narrative strategy; he offers Neil's first-person version of events. This narrative delineates a clear separation between Neil and the world he critiques. In Morrison's *The Bluest Eye*, Claudia, the narrator of record, disappears into the text, reemerging at certain crucial junctures. And in *Storyteller*, Silko's choice is even more complex; as narrator, anthropologist, poet, and writer of fiction, Silko moves fluidly into and out of the narrative. Yet there is a commonality between these three works. The narrators present their stories from a position outside and above the events described. Neil and Claudia speak from a "safe house" of memory while Silko positions herself as "the" storyteller, advising her audience

> the storyteller keeps the stories
> all the escape stories
> she says, "With these stories of ours
> we can escape almost anything
> with these stories we will survive" (247).[9]

In her study of elderly Jews, *Number Our Days,* Myerhoff noted that "storytelling was a passion among these people, absolutely central to their culture" (37). And Levi tells how, in Auschwitz "the storyteller comes in. He is seated on Wachsmann's bunk and at once gathers around him a small, attentive, silent crowd" (*Survival in Auschwitz* 52). The power of the storyteller offers these writers a measure of safety, marking them as different, powerful, and removed.

In *Goodbye, Columbus, Storyteller,* and *The Bluest Eye,* this choice of a pseudo-scientific narrative voice is reminiscent of Bettelheim's psychoanalytic observer. These narrators, as a rule, depend on self and deny any close identification with a group. But in *Portnoy's Complaint, Almanac of the Dead,* and *Song of Solomon* Roth, Silko, and Morrison invent narrators who are no longer able to stand at a remove. Indeed, in these novels protagonists search for a way to reengage with the ethnicity they have rejected.

In *Portnoy's Complaint,* Alex Portnoy questions the elevated position Neil Klugman promoted in *Goodbye, Columbus.* And this first-person narrator is no longer self-confident and supercilious. He is tortured and self abasing. In *Goodbye, Columbus* Neil never feels inferior to Brenda. He always views her from above. Seated at poolside, he even describes her as a drowner. Neil exhibits the confidence of youth. Portnoy is a different kind of man. Older, and ultimately more aware of how unwise he is, he longs for the country he cannot possess, the place where those Newark men throw baseballs and go home "gloriously pooped" (245).

In *Storyteller* Silko offers herself as the glue that binds a disparate narrative. But her narrator is an individual, blessed with good fortune; she is the one who escapes and provides us with her "best story" (247). In *Almanac of the Dead* Silko presents a world of disconnected individuals and provides them with an ambitious answer. The novel ends with revolution, those who are dispossessed managing to forge a pact, then rising up to overthrow the venal European-based society. These revolutionaries will remake the world in their own image. "Now it was up to the poorest tribal people and survivors of European genocide to show the remaining humans how all could share and live together on earth, ravished as she was" (749).

In *Song of Solomon*, Claudia's cool, self-confident stance is a distant memory. Milkman is a man who has little pride and even less self-knowledge. Milkman has been blindsided by his family's history, a history that includes Solomon, Solomon's children, and a bag of bones his Aunt Pilate has been carrying with her for years. Milkman spends years distancing himself from his family. But he discovers that his own personal salvation has exacted a terrible price. In the end he must retrace his family's steps and acknowledge his own link to its history.

The protagonists of *Portnoy's Complaint, Almanac of the Dead,* and *Song of Solomon* find comfort in their ethnic identity. They attempt to effect some sort of reconciliation through resurrection.[10] But this resurrection of a pre-disaster world is not wholly satisfying. Old concepts of family and community have been irreparably changed. These protagonists wish to honor their dead, wish to claim some connection, yet they are afraid that too close a connection will mean personal ruin.[11]

*The Ghost Writer, Ceremony,* and *Beloved* all make use of the same narrative device, a reanimated ghost. In *Beloved* the matricidal daughter must be vanquished, but other ghosts can remain to educate, to provide survivors with a way of permanently honoring the past. The ghosts in these novels demand sustenance, engage in sexual trysts, and become the object of parentally condoned lust. And these ghosts are allowed to say the unsayable. Amy Bellette / Anne Frank can proclaim:

> I wanted my revenge. It wasn't for the dead—it had nothing to do with bringing back the dead or scourging the living. It wasn't corpses I was avenging—it was the motherless, fatherless, sisterless, revenge-filled, hate-filled, shame-filled, half-flayed, seething thing. It was myself. I wanted tears, I wanted their Christian tears to run like Jewish blood, for me (190).

Nathan Zuckerman is not a Holocaust victim. But history stings. And he feels himself part of that history. He too wants his revenge, even though he doesn't quite deserve to lay claim to it, because he has betrayed his own roots. He is too American, too privileged, clearly not the dutiful Jewish son.

"A fully dressed woman walked out of the water. She barely gained the dry bank of the stream before she sat down and leaned against the mulberry tree" (*Beloved* 50). In *Beloved*, the invisible becomes visible; the unsaid is said. Sethe, a former slave who has killed her baby to save the child from entrapment, carries the dead with her, incarnate. In this novel Morrison revitalizes the past in order to offer a resolution. The village women must shoo the ghost daughter away to save Sethe and her living daughter, Denver. By acknowledging Beloved's existence, they integrate Sethe's act into their community, showing it to be one that was not just horrible but actually, spiritually regenerative. Beloved's appearance forces an approach opposite to the desire for invisibility. Morrison resists the use of the "mask" Henry L. Gates proposes.[12] It is a covering which he links to Yoruba ritual and which Gates deems a culturally accepted way of keeping the self hidden. Beloved's development into a fully fleshed-out person forces Sethe out of her protective cocoon. She is propelled forward into a community that has ostracized her. And this newly naked Sethe is finally accepted by those who have damned her. In accepting her, this society of women accept their past, their unlimited anger, and the impossibility of a real defense against the inhuman power vested in the slaveholder.

**Notes**

[1] Even the text of the book depends on a skillful interweaving of youthful memories with vividly described adult sexual escapades.

[2] See Mary Waters, *Ethnic Options*.

[3] Silko makes constant references to the Nazi heritage in *Almanac of the Dead*. And whites in her universe imitate Nazi behavior.

[4] In this way Silko echoes Bettelheim's critique of communal passivity. See "The Ignored Lesson of Anne Frank" in *Surviving*.

[5] In *Almanac of the Dead* our world teeters on the edge of destruction (as did the world of the Jews when the Nazis came to power). "When Jews in Germany were restricted to their homes, those who did not succumb to inertia took the new restrictions as a

warning that it was high time to go underground, join the resistance movement, provide themselves with forged papers, and so on, if they had not done so long ago. Many of them survived" (252). Silko's claim is the same:"All that mattered was, they were making preparations. When the time came, all these scattered crazies and their plans would complement and serve one another in the chaos to come. The people would be smarter this time" (*Almanac* 755).

[6]*Black Elk Speaks* gives eloquent testimony about the present version. "A long time ago my father told me what his father told him, that there was once a Lakota holy man, called Drinks Water, who dreamed what was to be: and this was long before the coming of the Wasichus. He dreamed that the four-leggeds were going back into the earth and that a strange race had woven a spider's web all around the Lakotas. And he said; 'When this happens, you shall live in square gray houses, in a barren land, and beside those square gray houses you shall starve.'" (9-10).

[7]Like Bettelheim's Nazi imitators and Lifton's emotionally tortured survivors.

[8]Des Pres, even as he argues against Bettelheim's vision of imitation of the Nazis, notes that for inmates in the death camps, survival often depended on fawning adulation and subservience. However, Des Pres believes that this adulation often masked subversive activities. Silko seems to have no subversive subtext. And she is different from Lifton's emotionally tortured survivors who are tortured by their adaptation of the oppressor's tools. She never pauses, never doubts, never examines her verbal strategy.

[9]The "we-ness" this poem depends on deception, for in the same narrative we find the storyteller claiming that her own escape is "her best story" (247).

[10]This is reminiscent of the way many *hibakusha* cling to their memories of a "golden age," a world of normalcy that existed before the explosion destroyed their belief in continuity. See Lifton.

[11] This belief can be analyzed in a number of ways, but the words Lifton uses are "death guilt."

¹²Gates says this mask is something "that is, covering the human face with an-other, second surface—to re-cover, in an almost mystical sense, a self-contained, virtually autonomous world" (*Afro-American* 90).

## Chapter Two:
## *Storyteller*; *The Bluest Eye*; and *Goodbye, Columbus*: Promontories of Power

Christopher Lasch believed that American society in the 1970's was devolving, becoming a place where we were "fast losing the sense of historical continuity, the sense of belonging to a succession of generations originating in the past and stretching into the future" (5). Leslie Marmon Silko, Toni Morrison, and Philip Roth are writers who have strong concerns with their own ethnic identity and the historical baggage attached to it. Yet each of these writers has chosen to present a version of self that is consistent with Lasch's diagnosis of the disassociated, narcissistic American. In *Storyteller, The Bluest Eye,* and *Goodbye, Columbus,* Silko, Morrison, and Roth invent narrators whose detachment echoes the separate positioning Lasch chronicles. However, these writers do not sever themselves from history in order to imagine an individualistic, hedonistic world. History forces them to choose between alliance with a group and dependence on self. They strike an individualistic pose in order to ensure their own survival.[1]

Silko's protagonist is the most autobiographical. She presents several versions of herself. She is memoirist and poet, anthropologist and fiction writer. Morrison's protagonist, Claudia. is our narrator, offering the story of a young girl's doomed identification with whiteness. Roth gives us Neil, a sardonic commentator on love and lust. These protagonists endure and often, prosper. In their ability to endure they stand in stark contrast to the victims they describe.

These protagonists reject the old-world communal version of ethnicity and the newer, homogenized, "Americanized" vision of self. They attempt to invent a place where they will feel comfortable as American ethnics and as survivors.

Many survival narratives end with a reaffirmation of the human connection. This reaffirmation can be either elegiac, a tribute to those lost, or an affirmation of the joy found in life now that danger is past. Whichever form this testimonial takes, it is something that recurs in narratives from disparate sources. John Neihardt's version of Black Elk's remembrance offers an elegant example (see *Black Elk Speaks*). Black Elk purportedly says,[2] "I did not know then how much was ended. When I look back now from this high hill of my old age, I can still see the butchered women and children lying heaped and scattered all along the crooked gulch as plain as when I saw them with eyes still young. And I can see that something else died there in the bloody mud, and was buried in the blizzard. A people's dream died there. It was a beautiful dream"(270). Black Elk identifies with the world he has lost, with the culture that has been destroyed. His own ability to endure offers him a way of addressing this tragedy, of remembering as survivors of the camps and as the *hibakusha* remember.[3] His words do honor to the dead even as they assert his own continuance.

*Storyteller, The Bluest Eye,* and *Goodbye, Columbus* offer an interesting contrast to this type of elegiac ending.[4] Instead of giving a testimonial that embraces connections, the narrators of all three of these texts glory in their own individuation.

All three of these works discuss ethnic separatism. All three address a history of racial and religious prejudice.[5] But these writers do more than testify. They use their ethnic history to induce us to believe in their vision of the protagonist as survivor.

Initially Roth, Morrison, and Silko respond to racist or anti-Semitic definitions of African Americans, Jewish Americans, and Native Americans by attempting to demythologize "whiteness." Silko's whites are one-note. They are physically unattractive, emotionally frigid. Morrison excludes whiteness from her narrative, preferring to condemn the disease of imitation that infects African American culture. And Roth depends on an absurdist rendering of the supposedly superior "gentile." [6]

In *Storyteller* Silko takes advantage of a scientist's detached superior position. She is the cultural anthropologist. Andrew Wiget asserts that because the Native American writer's audience is mainly Euro-American, "tradition can only be misrepresented. Neither can she [the writer], create something utterly Other from her historical and cultural entanglements . . . that space is occupied by Euro-American voices" (261). Despite one's best intentions, whatever the writer creates will ultimately become part of the "larger Anglo-

American discourse" (261). Knowledge of this inevitable cooptation informs Silko's choice. [7]

Yet Silko is adept at creating a dual identity. She claims she is Indian. Therefore she is able to deflect cries of racism, the type of critique that faces white anthropologists who spend their lives examining tribal societies. However, she also takes full advantage of her role as scientist. She disassociates herself from those she describes. In this way, she can testify even as she severs herself from the disastrous narrative she records.

Silko begins with her Aunt Susie, who was part of the last generation, a generation that

> passed down an entire culture
> by word of mouth
> an entire history an entire vision of the world
> which depended on memory
> and retelling by subsequent generations (6).

Jedediah Smith, one of the fathers of the Mormon sect in Utah, wrote, "On my arrival at the river which I named the Wimmulche (named after a tribe of Indians which resides on it, of that name) I found a few beaver, and elk, deer and antelope in abundance" (191–192). Smith uses an Indian name to register his claim to the land. His naming reconceptualizes the world. Smith usurps and re-creates, all in the same breath. Undoubtedly the Wimmulche had their own name for this river. Silko revises the conqueror's version of history. She takes back history, remembering the old names and reasserting the Indian belief that the whites were an Indian creation.

Aunt Susie tells the young Silko a story about a girl who decides to jump into a lake, despite her mother's entreaties. In the story, Susie returns to the old words to name the physical landscape.

> I'm going to *Kawaik*
> the beautiful lake place, *Kawaik*
> and drown myself
> in that lake, *bun'yah'nah*.
> *That means the west lake* (10).

Susie changes the naming order, replacing the English word with the native word and giving the latter primacy. She also places her depiction of the landscape in a historical context. Old claims outweigh new; the past is potent; the present is an illusion. As the girl makes her way to the lake and the mother pursues her, they follow a route that existed in prehistory, in the time before the incursion. *"There used to be a trail there, you know it is gone now, but it was accessible in those days,"* Aunt Susie says (13).

By beginning with Aunt Susie and with a story that serves vividly to mark territory, Silko evokes memories of a golden age.[8] Silko argues for a deep-seated spiritual connection between the land and Native Americans. Indeed, she offers this connection as one explanation for her own creative powers.[9] Silko believes that Native American's relationship to the land is timeless, whereas whites' relationship is temporal. Indeed, in her latest novel, *Almanac of the Dead*, a worldwide tribal revolution is staged to reassert this primal relationship.

> My great-grandmother was Marie Anaya
> from Paguate village north of Old Laguna.
> She had married my great-grandfather, Robert G. Marmon,
> after her sister, who had been married to him,
> died. There were two small children then,
> and she married him so the children would have a mother (16).

Here Silko keeps her narrative distance. She is simply showing us her family tree. Yet she is also pointing out the Indian sense of family. Marie Anaya, her great-grandmother, marries her sister's husband "so the children would have a mother"(16). The grandmother is selfless in her devotion, willing to take the place of a lost sister, willing to enter this union to provide security for the next generation. And she is also the Indian. This narrative ends with her great-grandfather "choosing" an Indian identity over a white identity.

> Grandpa Hank said that when the hotel manager
> spotted him and Kenneth
> the manager stopped them.
> He told Grandpa Marmon that he was always welcome
> when he was alone
> but when he had Indians with him
> he should use the back entrance to reach the cafe.
> My great-grandfather said,
> "These are my sons."
> He walked out of the hotel
> and never would set foot in that hotel again (17).

When Silko turns to fiction, the tone is more immediate, more aggressive. In the short story "Storyteller," Silko creates a myth. The unnamed Indian girl is prescient while the whites who exploit the land are unaware of their impending doom. The "final winter" is beginning, and the girl understands that they teeter on the precipice of a natural apocalypse (19).

But this girl is not Silko. And, unlike Grandpa Hank or great-grandfather Marmon, she is no close relative. Silko is an author here, distanced from the text through the act of creation. If this book were simply a collection of stories, it would be hard to define the author's position. However, Silko insists on including memoir, insists on naming herself the "storyteller." Read straight through, the stories in this book all argue against white privilege and power; all of them deconstruct whiteness. Yet she admits that she is herself part-white. Where does she place herself on her upended version of the Judeo-Christian ladder to power?[10]

Silko's persona stands at a remove for good reason. Although Silko evokes the "golden age," she does not re-create it. Instead, much of this book details reservation life, life in the gulag. Despite the morally superior nature of the Indian, it becomes clear that in Silko's world, those who identify themselves solely as Indians are doomed.

"Storyteller" is about the tensions that exist for an Eskimo girl who tries to straddle the white and Indian worlds—and fails. She lives in a tribal world that depends on mythic time, but she is curious about the more mundane world that has as its mainspring interactions with whites who have come north to drill for oil and build the Alaskan pipeline. In this story, as in the brief tale of the hotelkeeper and her great-grandfather, Silko's theme is the disparity between the morality, the goodness, of the Native Americans; and the immorality, the transparent evildoing, of the whites. This is an obvious response to the cultural and historical givens Paula Gunn Allen discusses: "No Indian can grow to any age without being informed that her people were 'savages' who interfered with the march of progress pursued by respectable, loving, civilized white people" (Hoop 49). But it is also an attempt to claim the high ground, the place of moral sanctity for the Indian.

The names in "Storyteller" are generic. The main character is "the girl." Her pseudo-grandfather, the man who donates the tale of the white bear, is "the old man." This old man is a link between present and past. He has been a sexual partner of the girl's grandmother and later on of the girl. He is also her spiritual guide, teaching her how to engage with her own ethnic history. He does this by relating the tale of a bear and a hunter, a hunter who "waited downwind on top of the ice knoll; he was holding the jade knife" (30). And he deeds this girl the power to predict the future by offering her this dreamlike tale of a "giant polar bear stalking a lone hunter across Bering Sea ice."[11] Once in possession of this story, she is able to free herself from the petty details of her daily life and her ongoing struggle with the Gussucks (26).[12] Owning the story allows her to take revenge on the white man.

"Storyteller" is meant to be read as a warning. Silko wants her white audience to understand the Indians' righteous anger, and its consequences. In this case, revenge means murder. But it also means that nature has sided with the Indian, that the apocalypse is coming. This apocalypse may be dangerous to all. Yet the Indian girl knows that a last winter is coming, and she understands that nature is furious with the whites; this last winter poses a threat to them because of their ignorance, because of their duplicity.

In this story, duplicity is part of the white man's nature. A white storekeeper has sold tainted liquor to the girl's parents, in effect committing murder. And when the girl sleeps with a white pipeline worker, she discovers his sexual perversity. He has a picture of a dog and woman coupling hanging on the wall above his bed. The girl makes no judgment on this picture; she simply notes that it is there. We make the judgment for her. And we understand that this unnatural act is another argument against white domination. It is a reminder of what should really be considered savage.[13]

When the girl adopts the role of hunter, the white man's sexual perversity entraps him. The lecherous storekeeper pursues her onto the ice and ends up tumbling to his death. Although he is not the same storekeeper who killed her parents, the reader sympathizes with this generic act of revenge. And the man she kills is racist as well as vulgar. "He remembered how she had gone with the oil drillers, and his blue eyes moved like flies crawling over her body. He held his thin pale lips like he wanted to spit on her" (29).

The girl is not only significantly better than the white men surrounding her; she is also elevated in her own community. After the old man dies and she takes revenge, the village people come to listen to her story. They carry offerings as if she were a deity. "At the foot of her bed they left a king salmon that had been slit open wide and dried last summer. But she did not pause or hesitate; she went on with the story, and she never stopped, not even when the woman got up to close the door behind the village men" (32).

By endowing this girl with the power of the storyteller, Silko gives her an acknowledged cultural position. In becoming a storyteller, like the old man, like Silko's Aunt Susie, like her grandfather, and most obviously like Silko herself, the girl takes hold of her responsibility as a tribal member. Silko states this responsibility baldly, in her poem about her Aunt:

> the oral tradition depends upon each person
> listening and remembering a portion
> and it is together -
> all of us remembering what we have heard together -
> that creates the whole story
> the long story of the people (7).

The story this girl tells is one of revenge, of retribution. The old man has warned her that "there must not be any lies" (26). The first lie means acceptance of a colonially imposed belief system which has granted cultural hegemony to the white conquerors. The second lie develops when there is an attempt to mask the righteous anger Indians feel. The girl responds truthfully. Rather than escape white man's justice, she makes it clear that the death of the storekeeper is intentional: "I killed him . . . I don't lie" (31) she tells her attorney. In shouldering this responsibility, the girl enters a dimension as infinite as that of the polar hunter in the old man's tale. She is the "legend narrator" Elaine Jahner describes, a storyteller who "generally views the subject matter as a validation of tenets of the belief system" (215). The belief system she espouses is one where the storekeeper's fall, the revenge enacted, is part of a reordered universe where Indians are in cultural and physical control.

Unfortunately, this deification of the Native American backfires as fiction. Silko's whites are too often caricatures; they are venal, predictable, and male. White's motivations are suspect because, as the old man tells the girl, white men have "the desire . . . for valuable things" and whites "hated the people because they had something of value . . . something which the Gussucks could never have. They thought they could take it, suck it out of the earth or cut it from the mountains; but they were fools" (26). Whites are like carrion eaters, they feed off others. They "only come when there is something to steal" (22). And they disappear as rapidly; the first storekeeper vanishes after he poisons the girl's parents; and the oil drillers are the most transitory of residents, working a job, then moving on. The white intruder is a blip on the longer Native American time line.

Despite Silko's castigation of white society, in real life she has managed to coopt the oppressor's tools. She is quite different from her nameless fictional heroine. The girl is wholly Indian. It is this that empowers her. But it is the white world that validates Silko; she is an award-winning poet, the holder of a Macarthur Award. The girl may be prescient, but she is also trapped. Silko, however, has found a way to escape. Yet none of the characters in this book are allowed the same ease of entry into the white world. Sollars's provocative argument for "doubleness" does not fully explain Silko's decision.[14]

In *Storyteller*, Indian victims abound. A poem entitled "Indian Song: Survival" tells of two young girls who have survived a flood. They travel high up in the mountains to a place where they turn to stone. The transformation of the sisters and the rest of their tribe into inanimate parts of the landscape reiterates the Indian's claim to the land. Yet it also illustrates how dangerous it is to be solely identified as Indian. These sisters are stone figures on the side of a mountain. The girl in "Storyteller" is going to be tried for murder. And when Silko remodels this legend of the two sisters, she further accentuates the danger.

In "Lullaby" Silko focuses on an act of murder and suicide. "The Wasichus have put us in these square boxes. Our power is gone and we are dying, for the power is not in us any more" (*Black Elk* 196). Ayah's life illustrates the effect of this loss of power. Ayah thinks that "it was like the old ones always told her about learning their language or any of their ways: it endangered you" (47). As the story opens, she has lived through the loss of a son to a foreign war, the loss of two other children to government medical quarantines, and the loss of a husband to alcohol. Her husband, Chato, has no self-respect because "the white rancher told Chato he was too old to work for him anymore" (47). Instead of attempting to seek revenge, like the girl in "Storyteller," Ayah chooses suicide. Silko elegizes this choice. Ayah's frozen death is noble, a self-possessed alternative to the degrading choices the white world has foisted on her.

Ayah is angry at Chato for capitulating to the white society, for teaching her to sign her name in English (47). When she comes to collect him from a bar where he has drunk himself into a stupor, she is "satisfied that the men in the bar feared her. Maybe it was her face and the way she held her mouth with teeth clenched tight, like there was nothing anyone could do to her now" (49). She takes her sleeping husband out to the rocks and wraps him in a blanket. Then she sits there, awaiting death. As she waits, she sings a song passed down through generations, a lullaby. What the words of the lullaby propose is a powerful connection between the land and her people:

> The earth is your mother
> she holds you
> The sky is your father
> he protects you. (51)

This is meant to echo what Paula Gunn Allen claims is a central part of Indian culture, "the basic assumption of the wholeness or unity of the universe, our natural and necessary relationship to all life" (9). Ayah has placed herself on a cliff. Once frozen, she and her husband will become like the stone figures in the tribal legend. Yet this connection with the past is tragic; her victory is also her defeat.

As she dies, Ayah's physical position seems even more intriguing. The text includes a photograph of Silko and her dog as an endnote. Silko sits on some rocks on a bright sunny day, they might be the same rocks Ayah has chosen, a place where "the giant boulders that had tumbled down from the red sandrock mesa throughout the centuries of rainstorms and earth tremors" are positioned to protect her against the harsh wind (50). Ayah freezes to death; Silko catches the sunlight. Silko's physical presence suggests a rather unsubtle argument against Ayah's choice. The idea that suicide is a way of linking with the continuum of Laguna culture is devalued, and Ayah's decision to embrace death is finally a defeat, though heroic.

Paula Gunn Allen proposes that Native American culture as a whole shies away from the notion that "a great hierarchical ladder of being exists on which ground and trees occupy a very low rung, animals a slightly higher one, and man (never woman)—especially "civilized" man—a very high one" (7). When Silko invokes the old stories, she argues for this, attempting to devalue the european notion. She says:

> you should understand
> the way it was
> back then,
> because it is the same
> even now (94).

Yet when she writes fiction, she cannot stop herself from reconstructing the same hierarchical ladder that Judeo-Christian culture has been imposing on Native Americans since the day of their first encounter.

In "Yellow Woman" Silko again gives tribal legend a modern-day guise. This time her Native American hero, Silva, is a twentieth-century ka'tsina spirit.[15] His romantic partner, the yellow woman, is a wife and mother who escapes from her everyday life into a dreamworld, complete with a handsome, sexually desirable outlaw as a partner. The modern heroine seizes on the story of the "yellow woman" as an excuse for her infidelity. But she also resists it, questioning Silva even after she has slept with him: "Who are you?" she asks him. "The old stories about the ka'tsina spirit and Yellow Woman can't mean us" (55). She is torn, unable to choose between an archetypal rationalization of her act and the more rational version. She has strayed because of simple lust.

Initially she tries to argue with his existence, insisting that "what they tell in stories was real only then, back in time immemorial, like they say" (56). He responds by pointing to the time outside of the European time line in which the Eskimo woman, the old man, and Ayah have taken up residence. Silva tells her that "someday they will talk about us, and they will say, 'Those two lived long ago when things like that happened'" (57). The woman understands that if she sees herself as a cultural archetype, rather than as a selfish, solitary sexual betrayer, her action becomes sacred rather than simply hurtful. Silva is certainly convinced as well as convincing. "What happened yesterday has nothing to do with what you will do today, Yellow Woman," he tells her (57). If that is completely true, then a revivified accessible past would offer a way to step completely outside of mundane concerns. But this woman's link with Silva cannot be maintained, because the white world enters the picture.

In a depiction of Silva and a white rancher who confronts him, Silko again delineates the repulsiveness of the European interloper. While there has been no physical description of Silva (what we get instead is his reassuring voice and the power of the woman's attraction to him), the white rancher has a "young fat face, . . . small, pale eyes" (61). Not only is this man corpulent, but "sweat began to soak through his white cowboy shirt and the wet cloth stuck to the thick rolls of belly fat . . . . He smelled rancid" (61). There is a stark difference between the elevated sensual pleasure that this woman has had with Silva and the physical reality of the grotesque white male.

Devaluating another through physical description can be seen as a response to the way physicality has been used historically. Descriptions of the Indian physique played a major part in the romanticization and subsequent dehumanization of Native Americans. They were "large, straight, well proportioned men. Their bodies were firm and active, capable of enduring the greatest fatigues and hardships. Their passive courage was almost incredible" (White 307). "The men are tall, large boned and well made . . . .They have a sound understanding, quick apprehension, and retentive memory" (Moore 12-13). Admiration for Indian physical beauty often went hand in hand with a castigation of their immorality: Indians are "savages who live in a rude and dirty manner, are of a darker complexion than the members of more civilized society" (12). And they are also "savage adversaries" whose "brutality and ferocity seemed to proclaim them a race of fiends rather than men" (Moore 108). Silko seeks to realign this vision of moral worth and physical beauty. This time, the "large boned, well made" Indian is the moral superior of the cowardly, rancid-smelling white.

Silko writes that there is something "ancient and dark" in Silva (61). Initially it would appear that this connection with the mythic Native American past is a source of power. Silva is a dynamic, winning character. The rancher accuses Silva of cattle rustling and Silva verbally defends himself. Then he sends Yellow Woman away and murders the unarmed rancher. The resurrection of this culturally potent Indian past means a readjustment. This time the white interloper will be threatened with extinction.

After the murder, Silva disappears and Yellow Woman returns to her family. Her tale of Silva's appeal, of his natural prowess, cannot be shared with anyone. No one is left who could appreciate it. Although her grandfather liked to tell her the Yellow Woman stories, he is dead (62). And her security depends on pretense. "I decided to tell them that some Navajo had kidnapped me," she says (62). Alone, Yellow Woman is unable to sustain her revivification.

Moreover, by giving up Silva's version of the story, she diminishes him. He is no longer a ka'tsina spirit; he is simply a murderer who has been angered by another man's racist assumptions. His act of revenge may be understandable, but it is also punishable. In the white world, Silva will be hunted down.

By offering her female protagonist this distance, Silko gives us some idea of how she herself has managed to balance the demands of the new world and the old. She can invent this supposed "tale of power," but she can also choose to separate herself from the act of vengeance. First, she puts herself at a distance. She does not see Silva shoot the rancher; she only hears the four shots. Then she invents a cover story, transforming Silva into a marauding Navajo.

Leon in "Tony's Story" resembles a totally modern Indian. He is self-assured, verbally secure. The female protagonist in "Yellow Woman" is self-confident and sexually aggressive, she chooses Silva as a verbal sparring partner. Leon offers verbal repartee to a policeman. And the policeman beats him for it. After the first beating, Leon is incensed. He claims that he has legal rights and says, "I'll kill the big bastard if he comes around here again" (125).

Tony, on the other hand, offers a different interpretation of the centuries-long conflict between white and Indian. "I couldn't understand why Leon kept talking about 'rights,' because it wasn't 'rights' that he was after, but Leon didn't seem to understand; he couldn't remember the stories" (127).

Tony is connected to the stories, to the potent tribal past. He dreams of "the big cop . . . pointing a long bone at me—they always use human bones, and the whiteness flashed silver in the moonlight where he stood. He didn't have a human face—only little, round, white-rimmed eyes on a black ceremonial mask" (125). Tony believes that this white policeman is an evil spirit, a part of the "witchery." [16]

Leon claims that the Indian is "just as good" as the white (125). In much of the story, Tony seems cowardly, obsequiously self-preserving. When the cop attempts to pull their car over, Leon keeps on driving defiantly, and it is Tony's voice that registers anxiety. He says, "Stop, Leon! He wants us to stop!" (126). When the white cop questions Tony, Leon throws in sarcastic, rebellious asides. When he asks for identification, Tony's legs are "quivering" (126).

Silko offers no psychological portrait of this white man. Instead she presents him as a soulless body, his eyes hidden behind silver-frosted glasses, Tony can find only his own reflection. To explain his aggressively racist behavior, the cop tells them that he has been "transferred . . . because of Indians" (126). His quest is messianic. He is after those he hates, and he will "find them" (127).

Tony's vengeful response resembles Silva's and the girl's. He must protect himself against this cop because he sees that "there's no place left to hide. It follows us everywhere" (128). Although Leon has spent much of the story making pronouncements about the power of civil rights and threatening violence, it is Tony, the Indian-identified character, who ends up murdering the police officer.[17] Despite his verbal bravado, Leon is terrified. Tony says Leon "kept looking at me like he wanted to run" (129). Tony, on the other hand, is cool and rational. "Don't worry, everything is O.K. now, Leon. It's killed. They sometimes take on strange forms" (129).

Indian-identified protagonists are driven to violence. Silko separates her own exterior narrator from these protagonists. And characters who resemble an assimilated version of self function as observers in this battle zone.

> a
> long time ago
> in the beginning
> there were no white people in this world
> there was nothing European.
> And this world might have gone on like that
> except for one thing:
> witchery (130).

According to Silko, the evil spawned by this witchery gives birth to whiteness. Silko takes a historic reality, the existence of native peoples in a continent an ocean away from European influence, and conflates that historical truth with mythical power. Non-white witches meet,"some had slanty eyes / others had black skin," and vie with each other (130). "They all got together for a contest / the way people have baseball tournaments nowadays / except this was a contest / in dark things" (130). At the end one witch stands alone. This witch, an outsider, is still clearly from a tribal background even though "no one ever knew where this witch came from / which tribe / or if it was a woman or a man" (132).

> This witch said
> Okay
> go ahead
> laugh if you want to
> but as I tell the story
> it will begin to happen
> Set in motion now
> set in motion by our witchery
> to work for us.
> Caves across the ocean
> in caves of dark hills
> white skin people
> like the belly of a fish
> covered with hair (133).

The witch's power comes out of storytelling. And the story told here is one of continental disaster. The whites are simple tools set down by this evil hand. The witch tells the assembled audience that they "work for us" (133).

> set in motion
> To destroy
> To kill . . . for suffering
> for torment
> for the stillborn
> the deformed
> the sterile
> the dead (136).

This mythical witch is another of Silko's tools. He or she enlarges the Native American's cultural hegemony. Whites are not just lower on the Judeo-Christian ladder than the Indians they have attempted to obliterate; they are so low that they do the bidding of this witch, the worst possible example of tribal peoples. And even the witches want nothing to do with whites. They agree that this witch is the winner of the contest, but then they say

> it isn't so funny
> It doesn't sound so good.
> We are doing okay without it
> we can get along without that kind of thing.
> Take it back.
> Call that story back (137).[18]

In Silko's myth, the unknown witch is given power to tell the horrifying story. His story of conquest outweighs all the actual horrors the other witches attempt. The reimagined history of white incursions is the most deadly act of violence.

"The Storyteller's Escape" offers the clearest view of Silko's individualism. Although she writes that "with these stories of ours / we can escape almost anything / with these stories we will survive," this escape is a matter of solitary survival (247). And it is the storyteller's "best story" (247). The protagonist in this poem has been abandoned by the people of her village. As she flees her enemies, she thinks

> this was how she would want them
> to remember and cry for her
> If only somebody had looked back. (249)

But no one does look back.[19]

It is the need to tell that fuels the storyteller's desire for survival. She believes in duty, in responsibility.[20] If she didn't feel the urge to testify,

> I could die peacefully
> if there was just someone to tell
> how I finally stopped
> and where (250).

Silko, like Sonny Boy, her modern-day Coyote character, is "good at making up stories to justify why things happened the way they did" (259). She has offered stories about racist incursion and cultural obliteration. Yet in the end, it is her own survival that is her best, her dearest story.

In *The Bluest Eye*, the dominant white culture makes its first appearance in the retelling of a primer story, Dick and Jane.[21] Morrison assumes that her readers are familiar with the illustrations that accompanied this series of readers, Dick and Jane as white middle class American children.

*The Bluest Eye* is a novel about the power of white iconography. Dick and Jane are an example of a grammar school discourse; young children were asked to identify with these "white bread" representations of perfection. Morrison offers us this instructional tale as a framing device and it stands in stark contrast to the story of her own protagonist, Pecola. Pecola is someone who drowns, pulled under by the weight of her own socially approved desire for blond, blue-eyed, white-skinned purity.

Pecola's story is presented by Claudia, the observer of the descent. Claudia claims kinship with Pecola but also stands apart from her. Claudia and Pecola's world is wholly African American. Yet Morrison chooses to frame their world with the story of Dick and Jane. In this novel, the white world surrounds the black, imposing its will from afar.

Despite her shifts in voice, Morrison has devised a completely experimental structure for this, her first novel. *The Bluest Eye* foreshadows the sort of interior and exterior wordplay she uses so skillfully in *Beloved*. However, the inclusion of Dick and Jane and the chapter breaks, the book is divided into the seasons of the year, offer a clue that she will eventually abandon tradition.

Claudia's voice precludes any notion we might have of maintaining a foothold in the bland world of Dick and Jane. Not that this is a complete shock, our awareness has been raised by the anxiety suggested by the typography of the preface.[22] Morrison's introduction of Claudia echoes Silko's choice of a more clearly autobiographical narrative voice. For Claudia effects a pose that closely resembles Silko's in *Storyteller*. Claudia is the owner of memory, the keeper of historical data. She has a mission. She needs to tell us the story of Pecola Breedlove, a daughter impregnated by her father, a girl who loses her baby and then goes mad. Claudia's decision to focus on this victim's tale mirrors Silko's focus on solely Indian-identified characters. And Claudia's distance from Pecola mirrors Silko's distance from Ayah's suicidal protest or the more violent acts of revenge undertaken by the Eskimo girl and the gun-toting Silva and Tony.

Claudia is the storyteller of record. She says "there is really nothing more to say—except why. But since why is difficult to handle, one must take refuge in how" (9). But the disaster recorded in this text is a something she has observed. She has participated in it up to a point. But Claudia is the survivor, Pecola the victim. So who is Claudia? Initially she does not seem to be the most reliable of narrators. Although she starts off the narrative in a youthful guise, her older (authorial?) voice intrudes, using an adult's terminology. "Being a minority in both caste and class, we moved about anyway on the hem of life, struggling to consolidate our weaknesses and hang on" (18). "Minority," "caste," and "class" are the words of someone older and better educated than the naive girl whose mother has taken Pecola into their household. Thus we are prompted to believe that this novel is based on memory . . . filtered through distance. Yet there is no clear indication of this. At the end of the novel, only a year has elapsed. And as the novel has proceeded, we are no longer even sure that Claudia is the speaker of record. We enter the minds of both the Breedloves, and ultimately, most critically, Soaphead Church. We realize that Claudia's narrative voice is used as a double for the tale of Dick and Jane. It works as the African-American version of that white framing device. Claudia, like the white world represented by Dick and Jane, is capable of removing herself from the narrative. But Claudia's world is a precious enclave of one.

Claudia stands at a remove from the black community surrounding her. She is the only one who really questions the pervasive identification with the white other. Indeed, Claudia is the only one in this narrative who does escape the destructive effects of racism. Pecola's mother and father are locked in a barren, vicious marriage created by their own difficult histories. Cholly, the father, has been shamed by white men, forced to make love to a black girl while they ridiculed him. For him, sex will always be mixed with unmitigated anger. His helpless rage forces him to turn against the women who accept him. And Pecola's mother buys into white myths of beauty, of propriety. She derides her husband while he attempts to subjugate her.

The prostitutes who live upstairs from Pecola offer her some limited acceptance, but these women are also victims, despised by the good women of this black community even as they service the good women's husbands. In turn, the prostitutes despise their clients. All these characters experience some form of social or internal isolation. For example, Claudia's mother is victimized. She is exhausted and overwhelmed by her hard life. When Claudia is sick, she says, "What did you puke on the bed clothes for? Don't you have sense enough to hold your head out the bed? Now, look what you did. You think I got time for nothing but washing up your puke?" (13).

Claudia is different from everyone else Morrison describes. And what sets her apart is a conscious pride in self.[23] When her sister and Pecola discuss Shirley Temple's good looks, Claudia is totally revolted. She hates Shirley because Shirley is the one who dances with Bojangles. Claudia expresses sexual jealousy rather than envy for Shirley's supposed physical attributes.[24] Her competitive sexual reaction is fiercely adult. When Claudia is given white dolls to play with, she is immediately aggressive. True to her critical, clinical nature, she spends a great deal of time disemboweling them.

*The Bluest Eye* delineates an African-American community of victims who prey on each other. This community in Ohio strongly resembles the world of the concentration camp. "In the Lager things are different; here the struggle to survive is without respite, because everyone is desperately and ferociously alone" (Levi, *Survival in Auschwitz* 80). Pecola and others languish in this loneliness, but Claudia glories in it.

Claudia's vision of whiteness is refreshing. According to her, Shirley is an impossible creation, "one of those little white girls whose socks never slid down under their heels" (19). Claudia understands that this white world, which her community is bent on imitating, is plasticized and precious. It is unsexual and joyless. Shirley Temple may dance with Bojangles, but her dance is a dance of denial rather than sensual pleasure. It is crushing in its bland stupidity.

Claudia's survival depends on distrust and dismissal of white values.[25] She is remarkably self-sufficient, disdainful of her community and its white-imposed value system. But Pecola craves attention, she desperately needs approval. It is this desire that undoes her.

Claudia adopts the scientist's pose. She is more of a surgeon than an anthropologist, working with her dolls to decipher the mystery of whiteness. She disembowels these inanimate objects because she needs to "discover the dearness, to find the beauty, the desirability that had escaped me, but only me" (20). Claudia's description of the doll is reminiscent of Silko's descriptions of the malicious whites who range through her tales. This doll has "moronic eyes, . . . (a) pancake face, and orangeworms hair" (20). She describes it as "aggressive" when she shares a bed with it, and it has a "bone-cold head" (20).

In choosing this doll as the earliest representative of white physicality in the novel, Morrison is invoking nineteenth-century scientific discourse, a discourse created because of the finding of ethnologists, a discourse which promoted the pro-slavery political agenda. One southern ethnologist wrote, "the negro infant . . . is born with a small, hard, smooth, round head like a gourd. Instead of the frontal and temporal bones being divided into six plates, as in the white child, they form but one bone in the negro infant. The head is . . . smaller than that of the white child" (Elliot, *Cotton Is King* 708). A century later, Claudia adapts this biased terminology. She replaces the African with the formerly deified white child. And she enlarges the scope of her experiment. She responds to the animate white girls she sees by taking the superior position of a supposedly impartial scientific observer. She studies their responses. "If I pinched them, their eyes . . . would fold in pain . . . their cry would . . . be . . . a fascinating cry of pain" (22).

Whereas Claudia is an interested but unscathed observer, Pecola bristles with scars. She is everyone's victim, everyone's scapegoat. She is both unloved, a piece of debris, cast off from her own community. Indeed, she is their most brutalized part made visible.

In Pecola, ugliness and blackness are inseparable. She and her family "lived there because they were poor and black . . . stayed there because they believed they were ugly" (34). Pecola's belief in her ugliness gives Morrison another opportunity to mimic supposedly scientific discourse: "The eyes, the small eyes set closely together under narrow foreheads. The low, irregular hairlines, which seemed even more irregular in contrast to the straight, heavy eyebrows which nearly met. Keen but crooked noses, with insolent nostrils" (34).[26] Morrison is certainly aware of the historical connection between hostile physical description's and social failure. "The master had said, 'You are ugly people.' They had looked about themselves and saw, in fact, support for it leaning at them from every billboard, every movie, every glance. 'Yes,' they had said. 'You are right'" (34).

Morrison has a great deal of sympathy for "drowners." When she leaves Claudia to investigate Pecola and her parents', Cholly's and Pauline's, interior voices, she offers poignant evidence of how they have come to their abandoned state.[27] Cholly, the child molester, is given a motivation and an excuse. She foregrounds Cholly's final, desperate act by showing us his shame after an earlier act of forced sex when he was a teenager. This loss of his manhood has haunted him throughout his life.[28] This one racist act, two bigots forcing him to have sex with a girl while they watch, distorts everything. He can never see the world the same again, and he will never be able to forget. Cholly feels anger towards these powerful white boys, but he redirects it. At first he blames the girl, "He cultivated his hatred toward Darlene" (119), and later on he blames his wife and daughter. Cholly thinks he understands the rules of survival because "never did he once consider directing his hatred towards the hunters. Such an emotion would have destroyed him. They were big, white, armed men. He was small, black, helpless" (119).

Pauline also lives in a "tainted" world, a world where she is unable to find comfort or acceptance. But the experience that rearranges her worldview is wholly cultural. "She was never able, after her education in the movies, to look at a face and not assign it some category in the scale of absolute beauty, and the scale was one she absorbed in full from the silver screen. . . . She learned all there was to love and all there was to hate" (97). On the silver screen, beauty is white and pristine. Thus, ugliness is clear, it is her own face and, worse, Pecola's.

Although the Breedloves imagine themselves survivors, they are clearly lost. Cholly is drunk much of the time; he ends up raping his own daughter. Pauline loves nothing about her home, idealizing the white children she cares for even as she dismisses her own. These parents are inhumane, if not inhuman. Their internalized anger destroys them. But Claudia refuses to internalize blame.

Claudia is the only one who is curious enough to analyze whiteness and disembowel it. The community that surrounds her is full of adults with an "unfulfilled longing" for the same dolls Claudia dissects (21). This hatred of self is so widespread that Pecola is right in believing that finding love for her "ugly black" self will take a miracle (40).[29]

Pecola will never be able to achieve acceptance. She is dangerous, her weakness a drag on others. She, like the weaker prisoners in the Lager must be exterminated. "Newcomers presented the old prisoners with difficult problems. A newcomer who did not stand up well under the strain tended to become a liability for the other prisoners.... To some it seemed as well to get rid of them" (Bettelheim 78–79). Pecola argues against her fate, attempting to counteract the blindness that afflicts people when they look her way. But she is fighting a losing battle. "How can a fifty-two-year-old white immigrant storekeeper with the taste of potatoes and beer in his mouth, his mind honed on the doe-eyed Virgin Mary, his sensibilities blunted by a permanent awareness of loss, *see* a little black girl?" (42).

Pecola's strategy is important. It is the most desperate example of the attitude her parents have incorporated. Instead of imagining herself victorious through an aggressive act, (such as dancing with Bojangles and murdering Shirley Temple in a culturally powerful celluloid recreation of an all-black romance), Pecola decides to change her physical self. She remakes herself with "pretty eyes. Pretty blue eyes. Big blue pretty eyes.... Blue-sky eyes.... Morning glory blue eyes" (40). Her choice of weapon dooms her.

> We took as our own the most dramatic, and the most obvious, of our white masters' characteristics, which were, of course, their worst. In retaining the identity of our race, we held fast to those characteristics most gratifying to sustain and least troublesome to maintain.... We were not royal but snobbish, not aristocratic but class-conscious; we believed authority was cruelty to our inferiors, and education was being at school. We mistook violence for passion, indolence for leisure, and thought recklessness was freedom. We raised our children and reared our crops; we let infants grow, and property develop. Our manhood was defined by acquisitions. Our womanhood by acquiescence. And the smell of your fruit and the labor of your days we abhorred (*The Bluest Eye* 140).

In *Sula*, Morrison offers sensuality as a weapon for truth; Sula's sensual nature is more honest than the sanctimony of her supposed best friend, Nel. Nel resembles Pauline, another straitlaced, churchgoing woman, and Sula's promiscuity brings to mind the easygoing sexuality of the prostitutes, Pecola's friends. These prostitutes are practical women. Their apparent immorality promotes acceptance. They are kind to Pecola. Pauline makes much of her own moral superiority, yet she pulverizes her children. "She bent toward respectability, and in doing so taught them fear: fear of being clumsy, fear of being like their father, fear of not being loved by God, fear of madness.... For her virtues were intact. She was an active church woman, did not drink, smoke, or carouse, defended herself mightily against Cholly, rose above him in every way" (102). Pauline's moral superiority masquerades as affection. She believes she is "fulfilling a mother's role conscientiously" (102). In fact, she is denying her daughter love.

Pauline believes that her morality will empower her, but she is mistaken. No real power is available to her through prudery. Her disdain is imitative, one of the oppressor's least attractive tools. "She needed Cholly's sins desperately. The lower he sank, the wilder and more irresponsible he became, the more splendid she and her task became. In the name of Jesus" (37). Pauline is one of "these particular brown girls from Mobile and Aiken" (68). These girls "are not like some of their sisters.... They go to land-grant colleges, normal schools, and learn how to do the white man's work with refinement, home economics to prepare his food; teacher education to instruct black children in obedience; music to soothe the weary master and entertain his blunted soul....The careful development of thrift, patience, high morals and good manners. In short, how to get rid of the funkiness. The dreadful funkiness of passion, the funkiness of nature, the funkiness of a wide range of emotions" (68). This need to eradicate the funk, this desire to obliterate passion, is an entirely destructive part of the slavemaster's legacy.

Pauline and her straitlaced Christian sisters perpetuate racist and stereotypical views of African-American sexuality. Pauline is sanctimonious about the prostitutes in much the same way that advocates of slavery were sanctimonious about their own supposed moral superiority to African slaves. The African "warrior would sometimes take a score of young females along with him, in order to enrich his feasts and regale his appetite" (Bledsoe 414). For the advocate of slavery, African male sensuality is linked to diminished mental capacity. For instance, the example just quoted is used to illustrate the "difference between a Hottentot and a Newton" (Bledsoe 299).

According to Eugene Genovese, "the Victorianism of Mamma and the admonitions of Missus did not always prevail against a thirst for life in a slave community that simply could not bring itself to decry love-making as a crime" (465). For Morrison, lovemaking is life-affirming; sensuality or "funkiness" is a natural part of an African-American's makeup. Any attempt to obliterate sensuality comes from a misplaced notion. Emulation of the master will not ensure survival. But tamping down sensuality perverts the affections. The end result is Cholly's brutal, drunken assault, Soaphead Church's desire for the companionship of pre-pubescent female companionship.

"I changed the little black girl's eyes for her, and I didn't touch her; not a finger did I lay on her. But I gave her those blue eyes she wanted. Not for pleasure, and not for money. I did what You did not, could not, would not do: I looked at that ugly little black girl, and I loved her" (143). Church's miracle is patently false. But Pecola believes.

Claudia wants another sort of miracle. She sees Pecola's child as the ultimate emblem. Pecola's baby should live to "counteract the universal love of white baby dolls, Shirley Temples and Maureen Peals" (148). Maureen Peal is the best example of the power of self-loathing. And yet, Maureen is the only character in this narrative capable of working a real miracle. She unifies the warring elements in her own community, enchanting the entire school (53). She is the physical embodiment of their most potent dreams, a "high-yellow dream child" (52) with "a hint of spring in her sloe green eyes, something summery in her complexion, and a rich autumn ripeness in her walk. . . when teachers called on her, they smiled encouragingly. Black boys didn't trip her in the halls, white boys didn't stone her, white girls didn't suck their teeth when she was assigned to be their work partners; black girls stepped aside when she wanted to use the sink" (53).[30]

Morrison deconstructs this miracle child, taking us behind the light-skinned veneer. Maureen is nasty and sneaky, entirely the opposite of her "Goody Two shoes" image. "I *am* cute! And you ugly! Black and ugly black e mos. I am cute!" (61) she tells Pecola when she gets the chance to openly despise her. Then she flounces away. Once again, appearances are all that matter. She wears Gates's conceptualized mask.[31] And she is deified for it; she is the African American version of the Mary Jane stamped on the candy bar, with "blond hair in gentle disarray, blue eyes looking at her out of a world of clean comfort" (43). Like Mary Jane, she is suspect, but only if you look hard enough, for the eyes of the girl on the candy bar are "petulant, mischievous" (43). It is more than unfortunate that Pecola sees them as "simply pretty" (43). That blindness destroys her.

In the beginning even Claudia is susceptible to Maureen's charms. She admits that she is "secretly prepared to be her friend" (53). But by the end of the book, she wants revenge. And Maureen is a stand-in for the demonized whites. For in Morrison's work, whites appear as minor supporting characters. They have a curious role, marginalized yet omnipresent. We are told that "nasty white folks is about the nastiest things they is" (95). The whites in the narrative act accordingly. The two white racists who force Cholly to have sex are only one example. A white doctor examining Pauline as she delivers, says, "Now these women you don't have any trouble with. They deliver right away and with no pain. Just like horses" (99).

Since, for the most part, white power is referential, the largely absent whites assume godlike status. But Morrison wants to obliterate the figure of that "nice old white man, with long white hair, flowing white beard and little blue eyes that looked sad when people died and mean when they were bad" (106). She presents Soaphead Church's alternative: the idea that this white man's God must be replaced because he has forgotten "how and when to be god" (143). The white Christian god owns "blue heaven" (144). He is a god who works miracles for whites and whites alone. It takes a black man to work a miracle for a black girl.

When Church donates blue eyes to Pecola, Morrison offers a bittersweet moment of hope. Could there be a universe that finds strength in the power of the usurper? Church has caused "a miracle" and has found "it meet and right to do so" (143). But his miracle is horribly flawed. Pecola is permanently removed from the community. True, she cannot be damaged by them any more, but only because she is so completely lost. Her blue eyes only serve to blind her to a reality that is, indeed, too much for her to bear. Pecola ends up mad, wandering alone. It is Claudia who survives, mentally intact and physically present.

For Claudia, survival depends on an acknowledgment of difference. Claudia is able to glory in her blackness. This alternative stands in opposition to Soaphead Church's sleight of hand, it offers a more desirable result.

In *Goodbye, Columbus,* Philip Roth appears to be dealing with a markedly different sort of exclusion. This text seems to be critiquing social inclusion and its attendant success rather than social ostracism and its attendant failure. Ben Patimkin is the "sink king." The reader is never sure how he has achieved this remarkable success, how he has survived so beautifully, for Leo, Ben's half-brother, a failure, complains, "I've got more brains in my pinky than Ben got in his whole *head.* Why is it he's on top and I'm on the bottom! *Why!* Believe me, if you're born lucky, you're lucky!" (117). The Patimkins live in a luxurious suburb while Neil, the narrator and protagonist, sweats out the summer months in his aunt's apartment in downtown Newark.

If chance alone accounts for the Patimkins' rise to the top, then they are no better, no worthier than the failures who surround them.[32] Roth subverts the Patimkins' specialness, their chosenness. When we see them through Neil's eyes, they seem decidedly mediocre. And dangerous. Roth focuses on Neil's escape from the "doomed" Patimkins.

The Patimkins are Jews made into Gentiles. In their newly founded kingdom, Brenda takes the place of the formerly powerful WASP princess:

> The first time I saw Brenda she asked me to hold her glasses. Then she stepped out to the edge of the diving board and looked foggily into the pool; it could have been drained, myopic Brenda would never have known it. She dove beautifully, and a moment later she was swimming back to the side of the pool, her head of short-clipped auburn hair held up, straight ahead of her, as though it were a rose on a long stem. . . . . She caught the bottom of her suit between thumb and index finger and flicked what flesh had been showing back where it belonged. My blood jumped (1).

From the beginning, Roth gives Neil the vantage point of a scientific observer. This whole description is distanced; the details are recorded for posterity. Brenda "dove beautifully" and held up "her head of short-clipped auburn hair" (1). We can imagine Neil seated by the pool, taking precise notes. Only at the end of the passage do we realize his own emotional investment, his lust, when he says that his "blood jumped" (1). Neil (like Claudia, like Silko) pretends to be detached from all that he observes, even though he is a supremely interested party. And Neil has to fend off intimacy. He knows that drowners reach out and take you down with them.

Neil wants to establish a safe base of operations. At first, it appears that all he wants is an escape from steamy, old-world Newark, a place defined by his Aunt Gladys. Neil relates tales of these pseudo-parents that are comedic, if one-note. When he phones Brenda late at night, his aunt asks him, "Who are you calling at this hour? The doctor? What kind of phone calls, one o'clock at night?" (46). Her overbearing concern and her implied Yiddish accent are enough to draw an image of a fleshy middle-aged woman. She is aggressive yet loving and involved in her community. She is like Myerhoff's elderly patrons of a Jewish center, whose lives revolved around a "dedication to social justice; they not only sought evidence of morality in a shattered, disordered world, but also worked to establish it" (25). But this community is dying off. Aunt Gladys and Uncle Max attend a Workmen's Circle picnic. The Workmen's Circle, with its socialist tenets, is the kind of unified community-based group that Neil would reject out of hand. For Neil is the consummate individualist.

There is no real danger that he will succumb. Gladys and Max are his aunt and uncle, not his mother and father. They are ineffective pseudo-parents who mouth familial concerns in a comical way.[33] They serve as decoys. Neil's directive, that he must flee them, is simply a conceit. Aunt Gladys and Uncle Max are ineffectual artifacts, dragged in to amuse.

David Monaghan believes that the central theme of *Goodbye, Columbus* is a working out of Neil's apparent "lack of commitment" (69). But this novella is not solely about the emotional shortcomings of its protagonist. It is also a critique of the idea of a neutered ethnicity, the cultureless self-empowerment that provides the fuel for the "melting pot." Neil argues against any emulation of the Patimkins. He offers a subtext: To go along with their sort of success is to create a family that is vacuous, cowardly, and even morally bankrupt.

Roth's choice of the first person distances Neil from all that he observes. Neil's sardonic humor is an integral part of his scientific stance. He describes and does away with his cousin Doris in three sentences. "Doris? She's the one who's always reading *War and Peace*. That's how I know it's the summer, when Doris is reading *War and Peace*" (7).

But Brenda is the perfect foil for Neil. To begin with, she is humorless: "Right from the start she was a practical girl" (7). And she is an imitation Gentile, cast from the *Mayflower* mold. Her suburban paradise is described, sarcastically, as one step "closer to heaven" (8). For this suburb has nothing to do with heaven (that is, unless it is the "blue heaven" Morrison derides). Brenda's Eden is soulless. It has "houses where no one sat on stoops, where lights were on but no windows open, for those inside, (refused) to share the very texture of life with those of us outside" (8). This salvation from metropolitan heat and squalor is soulless, a sanitized version of hell on earth. As Neil plays an endless game of basketball with Brenda's younger sister, he tells us that "the sun had sunk, crickets had come and gone, the leaves had blackened, and still Julie and I stood alone on the lawn, tossing the ball at the basket" (27).

Roth's disdain for Brenda is based on the same sort of complaint Morrison makes about straitlaced "brown girls" who sanitized funkiness. Neil's response to Brenda, a desire to fuck her, both physically and mentally, is thinly disguised anger at her attitude, at her denial of her ethnic heritage. And Brenda's decision to reject the sensual world Neil offers is an act of cowardice. Brenda needs social approbation.[34] It is this need that dooms her.

Neil is constantly, continually, infuriated by Brenda.[35] "For an instant Brenda reminded me of the pug-nosed bastards from Montclair who come down to the library during vacations" (11). Neil is angry because Brenda has inherited the Patimkins' overriding weakness; she believes in salvation through assimilation.

Neil doesn't believe the Patimkins have been saved. He shows us a family who are remarkably unappealing: the mother is devoted to artifice, Ron is vacuous, Julie is the quintessential spoiled brat, and Ben, the patriarch, is ineffectual and boring. Brenda is supposedly the most intelligent and compelling of this group, yet she is shown to be just as superficial as the rest. And they all believe that appearances matter more than substance. Brenda has her nose fixed; her brother intends to fix his.[36] They have sold their souls, and they have been given nothing of interest in exchange.

From the very beginning of the story there are clues to Neil's superior position. He sits at the side of the pool, elevated, coolly detached, while Brenda dives under the water. Neil is attracted to her despite her obvious shortcomings, "the smallness of the wings" (14). Neil engages with Brenda in order to prove his superiority. His victory validates his strategy for survival.

Neil is a heroic adventurer. He searches for a new world, a place where he can distance himself from the stifling confines of the old-world past as well as the Patimkin's sterile suburban world. His escape is impelled by a desire for sensual fulfillment and a belief that this fulfillment means real safety, real survival. Initially he thinks

Brenda will be able to join him on this journey. But that hope is dashed.

Neil's version of this new sexually charged world is clearest when he describes his "Negro" soulmate, a young boy who comes to the library and takes a book of Gauguin's paintings into the stacks, reading it with secretive pleasure. Gauguin's depictions of Tahitian women are rife with sensuality. And like Neil, this boy is elevated. He "likes them stairs" (60) which lead up to his secure cubbyhole. One night, sleeping with Brenda in his arms, Neil dreams of charting a new course. The boy is his shipmate. "I was the captain and he my mate, we were the only crew members. . . . We were anchored in the harbor of an island in the Pacific. . . .Up on the beach there were beautiful bare-skinned Negresses, and none of them moved" (74). Although he clings to Brenda as he wakes from this fantasy, reality intrudes. It is Ron Patimkin's favorite recording and the absurd chant "Goodbye, Columbus" pulls him away from these idyllic surroundings and back to the sanitized, suburban world.

There are temptations in this well-ordered universe but Neil holds out against them, employing his idiosyncratic survival strategy. Neil is the authority, the storyteller, the king of banter. He reconfigures the theatrical excesses of the Lower East Side Jewish burlesque houses.

Jewish law bars Brenda from receiving certain types of religious instruction. But Neil presents a new world, a place where Brenda believes she can remake herself. Yet she is stymied. She has none of Neil's verbal acumen. Indeed, she becomes his straight man. When Neil first suggests getting a diaphragm, she says, "Oh don't start that again, will you? I can't win, no matter what I say" (85).

Brenda's weakness can be read as a sign of sexism on Roth's part. But Neil believes that her craving for social approbation has doomed her. And Brenda's major motivation in life is fear. She tells him she is "afraid" of her nose (13), afraid that, once recognized as Jewish, she will lose the social position and privilege her family has given her. He says, "Why don't you have your eyes fixed" (15) and continues in this vein, adding that his cousin Doris is, "going to have her skin fixed" (16). When they do break up, Brenda offers his vision of her as an excuse for her behavior. "You're the one who from the very beginning was accusing me of things. Remember? Isn't it so? Why don't you have your eyes fixed? Why don't you have this fixed, that fixed? As if it were my fault that I *could* have them fixed" (134).

Brenda is right. Neil's assessment of her was immediate and irrevocable. He never believed he could change her in any substantive way. Indeed, if he had been able to mold Brenda, she would not have served her purpose. She stands as living proof of Neil's infallibility.

Neil's argument against assimilation bears striking similarities to Soaphead Church's indictment of the black community. Church derides those who have adopted the "worst of the slavemaster's characteristics."Neil castigates Brenda for remaking herself in the WASP image.[37] As he ridicules Brenda's attempt at assimilation, he sanctifies his own version of a survivor.

Neil's survival strategy connects sex with tenderness. In the library, his youthful sailing companion has come searching for the "heart section" (34). Neil's boss fears this kid's black funkiness, saying, "You know the way they treat the housing projects we give them. . . There is touching . . . and there is touching" (35). But Neil and his young stand-in rebel against these artificial boundaries. After sex Neil allows himself a moment of graceful acceptance. "She looked lovely, my Brenda," (46) "go to sleep, sweet, I'm here" (47). Neil loves Brenda most in that moment because, in expressing her own sensuality, Brenda reveals the one side of herself that has not been bleached into nonbeing.

All the Patimkins have this same Achilles heel. Their Jewish self exists like the refrigerator full of fruit, that secret place in the basement where Neil and Brenda "would fill huge soup bowls with cherries, and in serving dishes for roast beef we would heap slices of watermelon" (54). The preoccupation with food, with how much one eats, is a sign that the Patimkins are still sensual Jews. Ben thinks that Neil eats like a bird; Brenda shares her family's enthusiasm for ingesting; and Neil and Brenda's dates are an epicurian's delight, they inhale "corned beef sandwiches, pizza, beer and shrimp, ice cream sodas, and hamburgers" (54). The old model fridge full of nature's bounty is the Patimkin's link to their Jewish past. Neil notes that "this same refrigerator had once stood in the kitchen of an apartment in some four-family house, probably in the same neighborhood where I had lived all my life" (43).

Brenda's sexual intimacy with Neil is daring principally because the Patimkins have sanitized their sensuality. Ron's jock strap can hang in the bathroom, as inoffensive as a toothbrush. Neil battles against this by making love to Brenda in her parents' house, reveling in a version of a Jewish self which bears a striking resemblance to the Jew that anti-Semitic writers warned against.

"Jazz is a Jewish creation. The mush, the slush, the shy suggestion, the abandoned sensuousness of sliding notes, are of

Jewish origin. Monkey talk, jungle squeals, grunts and squeaks and gasps suggestive of cave love are camouflaged by a few feverish notes" (Ford III:65). But the Patimkins' musical taste would not betray them. Ron's record collection includes "all the Andre Kostelanetz records ever made" (64).[38] Neil feels contempt for Ron's taste. And when he describes Ron's one moment of intimacy, he goes further. Ron invites Neil to listen to his favorite recording, an absurd celebration of his college graduation. And Neil makes the historical link: "Finally there came a Voice, bowel-deep and historic, the kind one associates with documentaries about the rise of Fascism" (103).

The Patimkins have gone too far in their desire to merge. They have crossed over. They are like those old prisoners, accepting "Nazi goals and values . . . even when these seemed opposed to their own interests" (Bettelheim 79). And Neil is proudly, boldly different. When, during a moment of family conflict, Mrs. Patimkin castigates Brenda for inviting Neil, Neil's best defense is a personal acknowledgment of his uniqueness, "I sat down on my Brooks Brothers shirt and pronounced my own name out loud" (66).

Neil pretends to be envisioning marriage when he asks Brenda to get a diaphragm, but what he is really imagining is a place beyond the boundaries of both the old-world society represented by Gladys and Max and the new-world society of the Patimkins. Neil is searching for that tropical island where he can be like Gauguin, turning sensuality into an art form. His desire for Brenda to accede to this request for sexual protection is a desire for a codification of who he believes he should be as a Jewish-American. The request for the diaphragm goes beyond the "pleasures of the flesh" (80). For Neil, sexual intimacy and the attendant sensual pleasure ensure personal survival.

Leo Patimkin's life of failure is offered up as ammunition, a most convincing argument for Neil's individualism. Leo has to struggle daily just to get by. But he had a shot at salvation. As part of the verbal barrage that he throws at Neil, we find the story of Hannah Schreiber, a one-night stand who believed in "oral love" (116). Leo's attachment to this moment of sensual happiness is what links him to Neil. And his worldly failure separates him from the upper-middle-class Patimkins. Leo's fatal mistake was his abandonment of Hannah and that moment of sensual glory. His trademark line is, "Let there be light." Leo sheds light on the sterile morality that the Patimkins have adopted, a morality which confirms their view of themselves as an anglicized success (117).

Leo illuminates and Neil judges. By the end of the novel, we understand what was inside him "that had turned pursuit and clutching into love, and then turned it inside out" (135). It was his desire to prove himself a better American Jew than Brenda. He paints her as the true victim. Neil believes that sensuality pursued without guilt is not immoral. But Brenda is immoral because she uses sex as a weapon in the war against her mother, and because, in doing so she is denying her own passionate ethnic-identified nature.

Despite the clarity of Roth's vision, there are problems. Brenda, despite her supposed educational achievements, never rises above the level of a one-note, one-dimensional character. In this, she is unfortunately reminiscent of the rendering of whiteness (in Roth's case WASPishness), that Silko offers in *Storyteller*. In an attempt to give members of embattled ethnic groups a superior moral stance, both Silko and Roth end up demonizing their version of the cultural other. Morrison manages to avoid this sort of pitfall by choosing to exclude whites from the discourse.

Brenda may be limited, but her limitations don't excuse her. Her final betrayal is still read as a moral failure. Meanwhile Neil seems to have honored the power of his convictions. Perhaps this is why he sounds so confident when he says, "Brenda, the choices aren't mine. You can bring Linda or me. You can go home or not go home" (134). He knows how fearful she is.

Brenda goes home defeated. Neil is the conqueror, the survivor. He stands at the edge of a new world. Still, he is alone, a community of one. The Negro kid from the library has disappeared. Brenda has abandoned him. In the photograph at the end of *Storyteller*, Silko perches on the rocks, a smile wreathing her lips. She has avoided the pitfalls her characters have had to contend with. Claudia speaks over a distance; she too has managed to escape the boundaries of her own dysfunctional community. Neil accomplishes this same neat feat. He too is a privileged, lone survivor.[39]

**Notes**

[1] They mimic the detachment of Bettelheim's survivor, gazing back with a scientist's scrutiny into the sea of victims.

[2] There are valid questions about the authenticity of this document; however, I would argue for its continuing cultural importance. Most Indian autobiographies are, as Gunn Allen points out "not

autobiography in a Western literary sense. Rather, they are transcriptions of oral narrative in which the recorder/editor has shaped, consciously and unconsciously, the structure and content of the autobiography" (*Studies* 77).

3*Hibakusha* is the Japanese term for survivors of the atomic bomb.

4And here again, they echo the choice Bettelheim made in "Individual and Mass Behavior."

5Although *Storyteller* isn't a novel, there is no easy way to categorize it. It is partly memoir, partly fiction, partly a collection of poetry, partly anthropological study, partly an oral history.

6Another way of achieving equity is to elevate the victims. In their book *Race, Ethnicity and Society* Benjamin B. Ringer and Elinor R. Lawless argue that African Americans "angrily denied the contention that blacks were submissive and passive under slavery; instead they insisted that many blacks were hostile and rebellious and only the superior force of a repressive white society succeeded in crushing overt expressions of this antagonism. In a similar fashion many American Jews angrily denounced the contentions of Hannah Arendt and others that many European Jews passively accepted their fate under Hitler. . . . Ethnic groups feel the need to stress a heroic image of their past, as though such an image is essential for mobilizing their energies for the struggles of the present" (6).

7See Jahner on the tradition of orality. See Wiget for an intriguing counterargument. He notes that a discourse about Native American writing has often become a hunt for mythic underpinnings, a desire to ghettoize the writer. If this pursuit is carried out formally, it becomes "a kind of shadow anthropology" (259). I would add that for many ethnic writers, the act of writing is part of a much more basic and critical struggle. For them, writing becomes a way of authenticating personal survival.

8This is similar to memories of "both Hiroshima and concentration camp survivors, [who] in discussing their early lives, frequently presented images of a 'golden age,' of 'idyllic childhoods, spent in the bosom of close, harmonious families' "(534). Lifton argues that this vision is a way of reactivating "old and profound feelings of love, nurturance, and harmony, in order to be able to apply these feelings to this new formulation of life" (534).

[9] In a letter to James Wright she comments on this "very important dimension of the land and the Pueblo people's relation to the land," agreeing with his comment that in *Ceremony*, "it is as if the land was telling the stories of the novel" (27).

[10] Gunn Allen speaks of the Judeo-Christian ladder, contrasting it with the hoop, the Indian version of the world.

[11] The use of the bear has pantribal symbolism. See Parker for tales of the Nia" gwahe, "the most feared of magic beasts . . . . He loves to race and in various forms which he assumes, seeks to get men, and particularly boys, to bet their lives on the race, which generally lasts from sunrise to sunset" (*Seneca Tales* 17).

[12] Whites.

[13] Silko's belief in the corrupt nature of whiteness is one of the central themes of the fiction and poetry she includes in *Storyteller*. In this case, her belief in the corruption of white flesh does not undermine the effectiveness of the narrative. But in *Almanac of the Dead*, this theme takes on an obsessional quality, destroying the narrative flow and alienating the audience.

[14] See Sollors's proposal of a "double consciousness." This is useful in explaining the stylistic diversity in *Storyteller*. Sollors argues that this consciousness frees writers, alerting them "to possibilities of playfulness in establishing their voice" (252).

[15] "Yellow Woman went away with the spirit from the north and lived with him and his relatives. She was gone for a long time, but then one day she came back and she brought twin boys" (56).

[16] Silko's description of this policeman echoes one used by N. Scott Momaday in *House Made of Dawn*. In that novel, the main character, Abel, sees an albino who he believes is an antagonistic spirit. Abel notices "the strange excitement of the white man's breath . . . the blue shivering lips upon him . . . the scales of the lips and the hot slippery point of the tongue" (82). When Abel murders this man,

"he seemed just then to wither and grow old. In the instant before he fell, his great white body grew erect and seemed to cast off its age and weight; it grew supple and sank slowly to the ground, as if the bones were dissolving within it" (83). For Abel, the albino was a witch who had to be destroyed. He has cultural precedents for this act of violence. The same is true for Tony.

17 Tony's choice differs sharply from the choice made by survivors of the atomic bomb. According to Lifton, the "nature of the weapon makes specific revenge—that is, revenge 'in kind'—virtually 'unthinkable'" (534). Survivors of concentration camps also express repugnance. Jack Eisner, author of a survival narrative about camp life, is offered an opportunity to kill the head of the concentration camp and rejects the offer. He writes, "I can't go through with it, damn you, I can't be like you!" (304). For these survivors, preserving a sense of their own superior morality means rejecting methods used by the aggressor. In this story, Tony takes up the same weapons as the cop. Leon more closely resembles someone like Eisner.

18 Handsome Lake, the Seneca leader and holy man had a series of visions. The most potent of them also sought to trap whites inside of the Indian world. In Handsome Lake's vision he meets Jesus. Jesus "reported that his people had slain him in their pride and that he would not return to help them until the 'earth passes away.'" He asked Handsome Lake how the Indians received his teachings. When Handsome Lake said that half his people believed in him, Jesus declared, "You are more successful than I for some believe in you but none in me. I am inclined to believe that in the end it will be so with you . . . tell your people they will become lost when they follow the ways of the white man" (Wallace 244).

Handsome Lake assumes power by respecting and denying the Christian god. In another vision, he upends the folktale view of Columbus as discoverer. Columbus listens to the counsel of someone he believes is a wise and holy man. The man tells him, "A great reward is yours if you enter into my plans and carry them out. Here are five things. Carry them over to the people across the ocean and you shall never want for wealth, position or power. Take these cards, this money, this fiddle, this whiskey and this water" (384). Columbus listens to the advice and brings these five sources of corruption to America, and the Indian culture is destroyed. In Handsome Lake's story, as in the story of witchery, even those who are evil repent. The man who tempts Columbus is "the devil and when afterward he saw what his words had done he said that he had made a great mistake and even he lamented that his evil had been so enormous" (Parker 384-385).

There is oral testimony that also attempts to frame the history of white conquest. Dan Katchongva, a Hopi spiritual leader, testified at a Congressional hearing in 1955 that "in ancient times it was prophesied by our forefathers that this land would be occupied by the Indian people and then from somewhere a White Man would come .... We knew that the White Man will search for the things that look good to him, that he will use many good ideas in order to obtain his heart's desire, and we knew that if he had strayed from the Great Spirit he would use any means to get what he wants. These things we were warned to watch, and we today know that those prophecies were true because we can see how many new and selfish ideas and plans are being put before us. We know that if we accept these things we will lose our land and give up our very lives" (Nabokov 7).

19 This storyteller's plaint resembles the testimony of Holocaust survivors like Simha Rottem, who remember how at the end of the war, "I was alone all the time. . . . I didn't meet a living soul. At one point I recall feeling a kind of peace, of serenity. I said to myself: 'I'm the last Jew'" (Lanzmann 200).

20 Like Des Pres's survivor.

21 See Rosenberg for more about documentation on instructional texts. See Morrison, quoted as saying "all good art has always been political" (Steptoe 3).

22 Morrison begins with the traditional spacing, "Here comes a friend. The friend will play with Jane. They will play a good game. Play, Jane, play." Then she inserts a large blank space between this and the nontraditional rendering of the instructional tale:"Here is the house it is green and white it has a red door it is very pretty here is the family mother father dick and jane live in the green-and-white house they are very happy. . . ." (7).

23 This pride in self bears a striking resemblance to what Bettelheim carves out for himself in "Individual and Mass Behavior."

[24] See Kuenz for a well-argued interpretation. "Claudia hates Shirley Temple . . . because her socks stay up, but what really gets her is the presence in the films of Bojangles . . . the rewriting of . . . a historical moment . . . with her part edited or bleached out so that those few images of African-American life afforded space on the big screen are put there not as evidence or proof of the experience itself, but as a tactic for further erasure, denial, or revisioning of just that experience" (426). However Kuenz downplays the sexual or sensual nature of Claudia's interest in Bojangles.

[25] In this way she differs from those who survived in the camps, those "mussulmen" who became like their captors and found "by a miracle of savage patience and cunning . . . a new method of avoiding the hardest work, a new art which yields him an ounce of bread" (Levi, *Survival in Auschwitz* 80). These "mussulmen" were feared. Claudia stands alone.

[26] Set this against: "His lips are immensely thicker than any of the white race, his nose broader and flatter, his chin smaller and more retreating, his foot flatter, broader, larger, and the heel longer, while he has scarcely any calves at all to his legs when compared to an equally healthy and muscular white man" (Elliot, *Cotton Is King* 710). Whether or not Morrison was aware of this text, one theme of her novel is the oppressiveness of white-defined physical beauty. That cultural standard clearly has antecedents in the physical descriptions offered in these types of racist texts.

[27] See Samuels and Weems for a divergent interpretation. They believe that "Morrison's experimentation with the narrative point of view . . . muddles the degree of Claudia's success" (25). However, when one reads the novel as a survival narrative and sees that Claudia is the sole self-sufficient survivor, the delineation of other's failures serves to highlight her objectivity and resiliency.

[28] The concept of one seminal event influencing everything, forcing entire families and communities to obliterate themselves is much like Lifton's vision of the "tainted" world.

[29] In this novel, Morrison has little hope for the community. In *Beloved* the women of the community manage to embrace Sethe's

act of defiance, but here, there is no similar act of acceptance. Instead, at the end of the novel Pecola is cast out of the community while Claudia rises above it.

[30] Carmen notes that those who adopt white values are damaged in various ways, and he points to Maureen who is like these others "in adopting white values and standards of behavior, deny their essential value, subsituting false—even destructive—standards" (21).

[31] See Gates.

[32] See Novak for a counterargument, the Patimkins as drowners. She believes that "the world of the suburbs is larger than life and closer to heaven" (55).

[33] Halio offers a fine assessment of Aunt Gladys as "a model of common sense, hard work, wry humor and shrewd perception" who differs from Neil "in the depths and strengths of her commitments" (21).

[34] Like Pecola.

[35] Allen argues that "Roth's heroines do lack the quality that seems most important to him—genuine goodness" (146). This is certainly a valid feminist argument. But I would respond that Neil does not indict Brenda just because she is a woman; he indicts her because he needs her complicity. Though tempted, she finds herself unable to make that critical leap to safety with him. Instead, she does what so many others did, she chooses family. One notes Bettelheim's argument against this, his attack on the Franks. "Everyone who recognizes the obvious knew that the hardest way to go underground was to do so as a family . . . The Franks were unable to accept that going on living as a family as they had done before the Nazi invasion . . . was no longer a desirable way of life" (*Surviving* 248). Brenda is similarly deluded. She chooses to read the world in the old way. And she chooses family rather than permitting herself an escape route.

[36] This kind of decision mimics Pecola's pathetic desire for the bluest eye.

³⁷And by extension, the black community that surrounds him now.

³⁸Mantovani and Kostelanetz, Ron's two favorites, are known for elevator music, a version of the original that wrings out passion in order to create a generic and inoffensive product.

³⁹See Rodgers for an opposite reading of this ending. He believes that "Neil seems doomed to live the conventional life he loathes . . . because he does not have the strength to break free and explore the unknown depths in himself and others" (46).

# Chapter Three:
# Lonely Hearts Beat as One:
# The Importance of Family

Although the narrative structures of *The Bluest Eye; Goodbye, Columbus;* and *Storyteller* differ dramatically, the stances taken by Claudia, Neil, and Silko (the omniscient narrator of *Storyteller)* use the power inherent in difference. Each of these narrators creates a new version of a Native American, Jewish-American or African American self that is removed from both the old-world, ethnically pure community and the Americanized ethnic community, with its belief in elevation through assimilation. But this survivor's stance has one serious built in pitfall. It is emotionally isolating.

*Song of Solomon, Almanac of the Dead,* and *Portnoy's Complaint* are novels that examine loneliness. A longing for community leads to the resurrection of an ethnic communal spirit. Change is effected through engagement with the past.[1] But in these novels, the communal, ethnic histories are stifling and dysfunctional, so Roth, Morrison, and Silko present partially idealized visions of the future. They create a place where family and community can work, sustaining rather than degrading the individual.[2]

Although *Portnoy's Complaint* has been examined as a Freudian text, it is also, quite obviously, a critique of cultural strictures. Roth says that "Portnoy's pains arise out of his refusal to be bound any longer by taboos which, rightly or wrongly, *he* experiences as diminishing and unmanning" (*Reading Myself* 19). When the novel was published, the outraged response to this unexpurgated analysand's confession was any author's dream. The Jewish community was split, some castigating Roth, others applauding his honesty. [3]

Now, the novel seems tame. The world has become an overheated place, full of the most lurid public displays. Portnoy seems more naive than shocking and his pursuit of pleasure seems tragic rather than perverse. And Portnoy has other traits that set him apart from the many exhibitionists foisted on us over talk tv today: his guilt, his sense of humor, and his intelligence.[4]

Portnoy is torn between old-world Newark and a new version of self. His assertion of an individualistic identity puts him in a completely isolated position. "So alone! Nothing but *self*" Portnoy complains to his therapist (248). Neil's individualism was seen as desirable, powerful. But Portnoy has trouble finding a foothold on this icy precipice. Initially, Portnoy believes that he must separate from his family, from his community. He must protect himself "against becoming as they are" (Bettelheim, *Surviving* 52). But even as he pursues sexual and sensual freedom, he resurrects the past. His golden age may start out as a nightmare, but by the end of the novel it becomes a tantalizing vision.

Initially his mother is obliterating. And she is "so deeply imbedded in my consciousness that for the first year of school I seem to have believed that each of my teachers was my mother in disguise" (1). He flees her. Yet in the end his longing for the past is palpable:

> I sit in the wooden stands alongside first base, inhaling that sour springtime bouquet in the pocket of my fielder's mitt—sweat, leather, vaseline—and laughing my head off. I cannot imagine myself living out my life any other place but here. Why leave, why go, when there is everything here that I will ever want? . . . How I am going to love growing up to be a Jewish man! Living forever in the Weequahic section, and playing softball on Chancellor Avenue from nine to one on Sundays, a perfect joining of clown and competitor, kibbitzing wiseguy and dangerous long-ball hitter (243).

Neil never allows himself this sort of nostalgia.

Yet Portnoy lives out Neil's ripest fantasies. He allows Neil's vision of sensual power to run rampant, moving through Newark and through his family dinner like a steam engine. He describes himself as a sexual predator. But there is a gap between fantasy and fact. Portnoy's fantasy life, like the fantasy life of many teenagers and adults, is very rich. Yet his sexual experiences are fairly traditional. Although the Monkey permits him to live out his erotic fantasies, it takes Alex years to find her. Along the way there are plenty of Brendas to consider.

Portnoy's sexual coupling is an act of territorial aggression. "I assaulted and she surrendered. . . . What I'm saying Doctor, is that

I don't seem to stick my dick up these girls, as much as I stick it up their backgrounds—as though through fucking I will discover America. *Conquer* America—maybe that's more like it. Columbus, Captain Smith, Governor Winthrop, General Washington—now Portnoy" (234). Without question, this kind of reference points to a sexism on Portnoy's part.[5] In fact, Portnoy is the first to understand how unfair he is to women. Even as he spars with the Monkey and denigrates her, an interior voice warns him of the truth. "It turns out she is also a human being—yes, she gives every indication that this may be so! *A human being! Who can be loved!*" (194). Portnoy's shame is that he runs from intimacy, that he flees from the Monkey. And he does this because he is caught between two visions of the survivor's world. In one, entanglements are just that, tentacles shot out to drag you under. In the other, communal life is possible, desirable. Yet that world exists only in the past, in the "golden age" Portnoy resurrects.

Portnoy's diatribe against his mother is a sanctification. He notes, satirically, what happens if this exorcism does not take place. They end up like Ronald Nimkin, the quintessential Jewish mama's boy: "You couldn't look for a boy more in love with his mother than Ronald!" (96). Ronald takes his own life at fifteen, hanging himself "from the shower head . . . a note pinned to the dead young pianist's short sleeved shirt" (97). The note reads, "Mrs. Blumenthal called. Please bring your mah-jongg rules to the game tonight" (119). Even in death, Ronald is good, in fact, too good for this world. His devotion has forced him to commit the ultimate sacrifice.

Portnoy flees to avoid this same fate. He crosses the river and makes an Alger-like ascent.[6] He joins New York City government, becoming a successful member of the Lindsay administration. But his escape is brief. His individualism cannot really protect him.[7] Jay Halio describes *Portnoy's Complaint* as a monologue "about guilt-heavy, persistent, crushing guilt" (75).[8] Portnoy is riddled with survivor's guilt. He refuses commitment because for him the act of sex is the ultimate affirmation of life, and his "guilt saturated inner sequence" reads this affirmation as the ultimate betrayal.

Portnoy thinks he has found bliss with the Monkey: "it was suddenly as though my life were taking place in the middle of a wet dream. There I was, going down at last on the star of all those pornographic films that I had been producing in my head since I first laid a hand upon my own joint" (157). Yet he cannot escape the power of the past. Instead of surrendering to sexual bliss, he tortures himself. He wants "to save the stupid *shikse;* to rid her of her race's ignorance; to make this daughter of the heartless oppressor a student of suffering and oppression; to teach her to be compassionate, to bleed a little for the world's sorrows" (208). He wants her to feel as he does. If he manages this transformation, then he is sure he will be able to rid himself of guilt and possess the perfect soul mate.

Portnoy claims that he is unable to reeducate her. But we don't believe him.[9] This is the same man who told us that he sticks his "dick" up his girlfriends' "backgrounds." He has already made it clear that he is furious and that women are a stand-in for the real focus of his anger. Is he unable to transform the Monkey because he believes that "womanhood" should be defined by "acquiescence" (*Bluest Eye* 140)? Feminist critics would agree with this interpretation. Yet in the case of the Monkey, it doesn't quite wash. For one thing, she is acquiescent to a fault. She is willing to change for him and Portnoy acknowledges her attempts. In the end, he runs because he cannot commit himself. His guilt drags him back as he tilts forward.

Portnoy believes in social justice.[10] He hires a prostitute so that he and the Monkey can take part in a threesome, yet even in the throes of passion, he attempts to educate the prostitute, affecting a guilt-tinged, ineffectual concern for her well-being. "I couldn't believe that she had never heard of either the diaphragm or the birth-control pill. I told The Monkey to explain to her about modern means of contraception that she could surely avail herself of" (139). Portnoy is a generalist when it comes to human rights. He believes in "the rights of man, rights such as are extended in the Soviet Union to *all* people, regardless of race, religion, or color," yet he is unable to embrace a communal solution (73). He is repulsed by Israel, the ultimate Jewish socialist community. He cannot even maintain an erection in the "promised land."

Portnoy begins his survey of self by noting his physical resemblance to his mother. He has her "long Egyptian nose and clever babbling mouth" (2). She is so powerful that she "could accomplish anything" (9). And she is morally potent. His mother "herself had to admit that it might even be that she was actually too good" (9). Mrs. Portnoy can make things that defy "the law of gravity" (9). Yet despite her own vast gifts, Mrs. Portnoy has allied herself with a husband whose only real weapon is failure. Portnoy's father depends upon his own victimization as a way of giving himself some moral authority.

The older Portnoy has never been accepted by the Gentile insurance company he works for. He will ultimately be used and discarded, despite years of faithful service. This is not solely anti-Semitism. It is not simply that his father is "doomed to be obstructed by this Holy Protestant Empire! The self-confidence and the cunning, the imperiousness and the contacts, all that enables the blond and blue-eyed of his generation to lead, to inspire, to command, if need be to oppress" (38). Portnoy Senior revels in his failure. It is his weapon of choice, distinguishing him from the oppressor: "How could he enjoy triumph, when he so despised the triumphant?" (38). Alex's father believes that the moral high ground is held by the victim. His act of revenge becomes an act of self-degradation, but it is safer and more admirable than the alternative.[11]

Portnoy admires his father's moral strength and his implacable devotion to this brand of rebellion.[12] Indeed, Portnoy senior is a man in every way for "he was constructed like a man of consequence, two big healthy balls such as a king would be proud to put on display, and a shlong of magisterial length and girth" (41). But Alex wants success, not failure. He wants the power he recognizes in his mother, who "could accomplish anything." He becomes Assistant Human Opportunity Commissioner, a social service job by definition. This should be enough to placate the gods. Yet it isn't.

From his vantage point, Neil could examine two worlds: Aunt Gladys at home in Newark; and the Patimkins, ensconced in suburban splendor. Neil felt comfortably superior. Portnoy's escape is physical as well as mental. He crosses the Hudson, then flies west to Europe and on to Israel, and never finds a home. He lives with the conquerors, recognizing that they are untrustworthy.[13] Initially he adopts their values, taking revenge by cutting a sexual swath through the heartland of America. He "assaulted and she surrendered . . . on her mahogany fourposter (a Maulsby family heirloom)" (234).

Modern Jewish women have the ability to survive, to endure, without adopting the aggressor's swaggering behavior. Naomi, the Israeli woman he attempts to bed, is more clinically detached than any scientist. And she is refreshingly honest in her assessment of him. She slams him to the floor when he tries to come on to her, then tells him, "You are the most unhappy person I have ever known. You are like a baby" (264). Portnoy attempts to rape her, but that fails because he cannot maintain an erection. He grovels, begging to give her sexual satisfaction, and she offers a well-placed kick to the balls. Naomi is cool; Portnoy is full of whining heat. Naomi is a representative of the new Israel. Portnoy does not represent the old. Rather, he is the Jewish-American man caught between two worlds.

Portnoy seems to envision a society where sexual pleasure will replace ethnic bonding, where sensuality will define intimacy. At the end of *Goodbye, Columbus* we could easily believe in the existence of a woman who would understand and satisfy Neil. But *Portnoy's Complaint* offers a much less complacent vision of the future. For Alexander has found the Monkey. She is a woman who tells him "pick a hole, any hole, I'm yours!" (195). She is everything Neil ever envisioned, and more. Yet he dismisses her.

Portnoy realizes there is no way to replace the old structures or re-create the family life he has abandoned. "You don't know what you want me to be" the Monkey tells him (197). In *Portnoy's Complaint* Roth reexamines Neil's vision of freedom and finds it deeply flawed. For although Portnoy feels contempt for Jews, he hates non-Jews even more. In his friend's kitchen "tacked above the Girardi sink [there] is a picture of Jesus Christ floating to Heaven in a pink nightgown. How disgusting can human beings be! The Jews I despise for their narrow-mindedness, their self-righteousness, the incredibly bizarre sense that these cavemen who are my parents and relatives have somehow gotten of their superiority—but when it comes to tawdriness and cheapness, to beliefs that would shame even a gorilla, you simply cannot top the *goyim*" (167). He places Jews above Christians, even as he places himself above both.

In his savaging of others, Portnoy becomes less and less attractive to the reader. And Roth knows this. Indeed, his purpose is to make us critical of Portnoy, critical of his need to cling to this place of safety. Portnoy admits his own cowardice. When he rejects the Monkey because she has prostituted herself in the past, his sarcastic riff makes his own self-loathing clear. "Ah, but there is (let us bow our heads), there is 'my dignity' to consider, my good name. What people will think. . . . This girl once did it *for money* " (199).

We understand a truth that Alexander must ignore. The Monkey is simply another version of Portnoy. She is as gifted at disguise as he is. The Monkey has "the hillbilly routine, the Betty-Boop-dumb-cunt routine, the teeny-bopper bit" (196). She can assume the guise of a sexual boy-toy but she can also act surprisingly intelligent and unaffected. And Portnoy is just as chameleon-like. He is the good Jewish boy who "in honor of his courageous stand against bigotry and hatred, was invited to the Essex House in Newark to attend the convention of the C.I.O. Political Action Committee. . . . who skipped two grades of grammar school" (129).

He is the one who "in 1946, because they wouldn't let Marian Anderson sing in Convention Hall . . . led my entire eighth-grade class in refusing to participate in the annual patriotic-essay contest sponsored by the D.A.R." (129). And he is also the kid who "fucked my own family's dinner" (133). This ability to shift persona, to disguise the self, is a central part of the survivor's personality.[14] Des Pres characterizes this as "the duality of behavior in extremity" (117).

This chameleon-like behavior may save them, but it doesn't lead to the forging of a long-term bond. Like Portnoy, the Monkey has been unsuccessful in forming long-term intimate attachments. She has been through marriage and sexual manipulation. However, when he meets her, she is on the cusp of change and desperate for something more. We get to judge her desperation from afar, through his eyes, as something pathetic. She calls him constantly. He finds this embarrassing. She picks the largely unavailable Portnoy and tries to cling. He shoves her aside without admitting how much her survival strategy resembles his own. She would like to "not have to go back" to the unsatisfactory world she has invented (195). She says, "Wouldn't it be nice someday to live in the country with someone you really liked" (195). The Monkey is ultimately more courageous than Portnoy, for she is willing to shed the ability to live solo. She wants to believe in a world where someone can be trusted.

Portnoy refuses to trust. He idealizes the old world, claiming "I love those men! I want to grow up to *be* one of those men! To be going home to Sunday dinner at one o'clock, sweat socks pungent from twenty-one innings of softball . . . a robust Jewish man now gloriously pooped—yes, home I head for resuscitation . . . and to whom? To *my* wife and *my* children, to a family of my own. . . . Hard work in an idealistic profession; games played without fanaticism and violence, games played among like-minded people, and with laughter; and family forgiveness and love" (245-247). The sharpness of his pain is as much a surprise to Portnoy as it is to us. "How could I be feeling a wound in a place where I was not even vulnerable?" he asks (230). By returning to childhood images and coating them with a softened, romanticized glaze, he purports to have changed his perception of the things he has abandoned. Still, he can never return. That world is shattered. "What has become of my purposes. . . Home? I have none. Family? No," he moans (248).

Portnoy's future is bleak. Non-Jews are suspect, but Jewish women are too much like that prestidigitator he has admired, flinging glances at her over his shoulder as he sped away. According to Portnoy, Naomi is "my mother" (258). Bedding her would mean breaking the most central of all Freudian taboos. Worse, it would emasculate him. Sexual congress and a long-term sexual union with a Jewish woman mean taking up where his father left off. He would be forced into adopting the self-defeating behavior his father saw as a badge of courage. He would be barred from achieving success, which is the most American form of salvation.

Naomi describes Israel as a place where "the system is humane and just," where "the community owns the means of production," where "all needs are provided by the community, [and] as long as no man has the opportunity to accumulate wealth or to live off the surplus value of another man's labor, then the essential character of the kibbutz is being maintained" (262–263). This textbook definition of life on a cooperative farm echoes Alex's teenage pro-communist stance. But Alex is no longer an idealistic teenager; he is an adult, an American. Naomi defines America from the Israeli's perspective, a place that fosters "rivalry, competition, envy, jealousy, all that is malignant in human character" (261).[15] Alex cannot buy into this relentlessly negative vision.

Roth courts his audience by making Naomi's version of Jewish socialism dogmatic and crisply utilitarian. She is efficient and humorless, while Portnoy is all soul, all tortured heart. He cannot exist in this perfectly ordered environment. For there is nothing tidy in the psyche of a survivor.

Portnoy is a man with no way out. He has tried Neil's version of a new world plan and found it wanting. Yet he cannot invent a new philosophy that embraces old-world and new-world values. So instead of Neil's supercilious confidence, we get Alex's self-flagellation, his despair, his howl.

Portnoy Senior is an unsuccessful insurance agent, a lowly foot soldier for a WASP conglomerate. An insurance salesman also plays a key role in *Song of Solomon*. As *Song of Solomon* opens, Robert Smith, an agent for the North Carolina Mutual Life Insurance, decides to fly "from Mercy [Hospital] to the other side of Lake Superior" (3). He leaps and finds that air alone cannot sustain him. As he crashes to the ground, a pregnant woman watches him. A day later, her child is born, Milkman Dead. Milkman is the first black child born in Mercy hospital.

In this novel Smith's attempt at flight is a way of referring to time and circumscribing failure. Smith discovers that "only birds and airplanes could fly" (9). This discovery "saddened him and left his imagination so bereft that he appeared dull even to the women who did not hate his mother" (9). Smith plummets like Icarus, and this novel adapts the formal structure of the questing myth, with Milkman as the hero. His birth has been marked by this signal event, Robert Smith's aborted attempt at flight. And his birth is special in another way; he integrates a formerly segregated hospital ward.

Alex Portnoy and Milkman Dead would seem to have little in common. Portnoy is a middle-class Jew, a man obsessed with words, man who luxuriates in complaint. Milkman is a middle-class black who is secretive, often silent. Yet both men are lonely and fearful. Both attempt to find relief through an examination of history.

In *Portnoy's Complaint*, Alex longed for a way to make a connection with his past that wouldn't endanger him. But Alex could not reenter the ordered old-world universe. However, Milkman's survival depends on a revivification of this past. He needs to have the "golden age" back. When Milkman discovers his people, he feels "as excited as a child confronted with boxes and boxes of presents under the skirt of a Christmas tree. Somewhere in the pile was a gift for him" (308). Milkman needs to understand his history in order to soar.[16] If he attempts to take off without realizing that "if you surrendered to the air, you could *ride* it," he, like Smith before him, will plunge to earth, a goner (341).

In this novel Morrison presents a family so richly dysfunctional that it makes the Breedloves seem normal. And this novel offers a further indictment of the splintered black community. The protagonist, Milkman, depends on a lack of connection, a dissociation from the world around him. In this, he imitates his family's distance from the community. Milkman's grandfather was a middle class black man with an upper-class attitude. His mother carries on in that vein; she lives in her father's house, a "big dark house of twelve rooms" (9). She has afternoon tea, a formal English habit. And she believes in having a centerpiece, "always something to grace the dinner table in the evening" for "it was for her father a touch that distinguished his own family from the people among whom they lived" (12). His father's real estate holdings further cement the family's status. It is different from and better than the rest.

But Milkman's self-protectiveness eventually turns to scorn. He needs to escape from his family because he recognizes what others in the community also know, "that the house was more prison than palace" (9). Claudia was powerful, self-confident, and a spokeswoman for Pecola. She was the only one in her community who wanted Pecola's child to live. She saw Pecola as a victim who deserved support and salvation. Milkman feels no such sympathy for anyone. His major motivation is fear rather than anger. This motivation is behind his purposeful inability to connect with family and lovers. He is afraid of their power to pull him back into the world of the dead. His disaffection betrays itself in his emotional carelessness. And emotionally careless people are dangerous.

Milkman desires a separation from his mother because she nursed him "until I was . . . old. Too old" (126). He needs to be rid of her in the way that Alex needs to be rid of Mrs. Portnoy. But his mother needs intimacy to sustain herself, and when he rejects her, she burrows inward. Finally, the only one she can talk to is her dead father. Milkman also betrays Hagar, a woman who loves him passionately. His rejection sends her into a downward spiral that ends in death. These two women need someone to belong to, someone who can sustain them through a process of symbiosis. Guitar, Milkman's best friend, tries to educate Hagar. He says, "It's a bad word, 'belong.' Especially when you put it with somebody you love. Love shouldn't be like that. Did you ever see the way the clouds love a mountain? They circle all around it; sometimes you can't even see the mountain for the clouds. But you know what? You go up top and what do you see? His head. The clouds never cover the head. . . . You can't own a human being. You can't lose what you don't own" (309–310). Milkman flees because he is afraid of being enfolded. Yet he still yearns for some sort of closeness, some communal feeling.

Milkman's family is so oppressive and the community he lives in is so bereft that we side with his desire for escape. After all, he is surrounded by the living Dead. His father, Macon, is a man cut off from family and community, a man whose faith revolves around acquisition. He has certainly taken the worst of the white man's inheritance as his own. And he has done this because he has misread history. Macon Dead's father was murdered by greedy whites. Then they took over his piece of prime southern real estate. Macon becomes a landlord to correct this injustice. But you can't right a wrong through imitation. His revenge turns into a black-on-black version of the white-on-black crime.

Milkman cannot depend on Macon for emotional sustenance, so he turns elsewhere. But his best friend, Guitar, joins the Seven Days, a group that commits random murders to redress the historical imbalance, innocent whites for innocent blacks. Milkman can't agree with that coldhearted philosophy. Milkman wants to reinvent justice. And he longs for an intimacy that's safe rather than suicidal. But "deep down in that pocket where his heart hid, he felt used. Somehow everybody was using him for something or as something. Working out some scheme of their own on him, making him the subject of their dreams" (165–166).

In her description of the Deads, Morrison returns to her indictment of the holier-than-thou "brown girls" from Aiken. The Dead's middle-class morality condemns sensuality, yet they, like those Aiken girls, have untapped longings which end up being twisted into "dirty" sexual desire. In *The Bluest Eye* Cholly's sexuality was thwarted. He was humiliated by the white men who forced him into an act of sexual congress. And he was frustrated by his wife, who made him feel stupid, small, and dirty. He turned these frustrations around and found drunken intimacy with his daughter. In *Song of Solomon*, incest also plays a central role. Class makes a difference, though. While Pecola wanders the streets, an obvious victim of parental abuse, Ruth, Milkman's mother, lives in middle-class comfort, her longing for her father a well-kept secret. This longing simmers for years, fueling the furious disapproval that will energize Macon.

Her love for her father comes out of a tamping down of her own sensuality. And it is laid bare by Macon, who discovers her with her dead father. Ruth is "sucking his fingers, and if she do that when he was dead, what'd she do when he was alive" (74). When Macon discovers Ruth's passion, he doesn't question its source, and he doesn't use it as a way of achieving intimacy. It becomes his secret too, a weapon to be wielded against her for the rest of their married life.

Macon enjoys his power over Ruth. He will not permit her to expunge the past.[17] "What might hide this single flaw on the splendid wood: Vaseline, tobacco juice, iodine, sanding followed by linseed oil. She had tried them all. But her glance was nutritious; the spot became, if anything, more pronounced as the years passed" (11). This desire to continue his punishment of his wife is part of Macon's misreading of an acceptable survival strategy. He thinks that in this way he can purge his own fury. But he is only adopting the straitlaced Christian values of the master race.

Macon isn't the only one who ostracizes Ruth. Her longing for intimacy is apparent in her breast-feeding of her son, but once that act becomes public, it is ridiculed. She becomes a social outcast, like Pecola. And in denying her need, her passion, Ruth denies the most primary part of herself. Ruth's sensuality is not sinful, but it has been twisted by years of unredeemed longing. What began as a need for intimate connection has become something most peculiar. She explains this to Milkman when she describes her attachment to her father: "I had no friends, only schoolmates who wanted to touch my dresses and my white silk stockings. But I didn't think I'd ever need a friend because I had him. . . . When he left . . . I kept on reigniting that cared-for feeling that I got from him" (124).

The Deads are not a family at all; they are tenants of the same house, thrown together by chance, their only obvious link, the last name they share. And this last name is a mistake, a gift from an uninterested white man.[18] Macon Dead's mother, Sing, had a strong belief in the power of assimilation. Sing's misguided belief seals her family's doom. Macon's "own parents . . . had agreed to abide by a naming done to them by somebody who couldn't have cared less. Agreed to take and pass on to all their issue this heavy name scrawled in perfect thoughtlessness by a drunken Yankee in the Union Army" (18). Macon tells Milkman that "Mama liked it. Liked the name. Said it was new and would wipe out the past" (54).[19] But this new name does nothing to eradicate racism. Sing dies in childbirth; her husband dies protecting his property; her children move north and live estranged from each other and from their own black community. And they are bearers of this name, inheritors of this reminder of Sing's deluded belief.

In an attempt to overturn the white man's power to name and rename, Milkman is named by the black community. This nickname, given to him when he is discovered sipping his mother's milk past the socially accepted age, is community-sponsored; his last is a by product of a white man's lack of interest. The two names stand in opposition to each other. Dead is the name given to them by a careless white bureaucracy. But Milkman is a nickname that will stand as a symbol of all that his mother and others in the family have denied. The name betrays the power of their hidden sensuality, the power of their true heritage.

Macon Dead attempts to deny his past. Then he becomes as avaricious as the murderous Butlers. Instead of facing his own anger, Macon buries it. His father's murder impels him toward this eradication of his own personal history. Macon advises Milkman to "own things. And let the things you own own other things. Then you'll own yourself and other people too" (55). But Morrison has contempt for his decision, even as she has sympathy for the loss this character experiences. She makes it clear that she disagrees with any attempt to hide the past. Yet even though she calls for a close examination of African-American's victimization, she does not brook revenge against the white establishment. Instead, she offers a stinging indictment of that way of coming to terms with racism. She does this in her complicated portrait of Guitar, Milkman's best friend.

Twelve-year-old Milkman meets Guitar at school. Guitar is "the boy who not only could liberate him, but could take him to the woman who had as much to do with his future as she had his past" (35). Guitar introduces him to Pilate, his father's sister. Initially Guitar appears to be Milkman's soul mate. And when Milkman complains that he doesn't like his name, Guitar tells him, "Niggers get their names the way they get everything else—the best way they can" (88). Milkman asks why African-Americans can't get their names the right way, and Guitar argues that "the best way is the right way" (88). Yet Guitar veers away from Milkman; and when Milkman says that Guitar reminds him of Malcolm X, Guitar shows his own blindness about naming and the power inherent in this seemingly whimsical act.

> "You sound like that red-headed Negro named X. Why don't you join him and call yourself Guitar X?"
> "X, Bains-what difference does it make? I don't give a damn about names."
> "You miss the point. His point is to let white people know you don't accept your slave name" (161).

Although Milkman and Guitar are contemporaries, Guitar's emotional makeup is like Macon Dead's. Like Macon, he avoids commitment. And he too develops a self- protectiveness based on this early loss. Guitar's father dies performing menial labor for a white mill owner: "My father got sliced up in a sawmill and his boss came by and gave us kids some candy" (61). Now Guitar equates candy with nausea, and with the whites who gave him this condescending version of comfort. Guitar says that "everything I ever loved in my life left me" (311). His response to this is to divorce himself emotionally, because "if I loved anything it would die" (311).

Guitar devotes himself to revenge. When Milkman asks him why kill innocent people, he says, "Each and every one of them could do it. So you just get any one of them. There are no innocent white people, because every one of them is a potential nigger-killer, if not an actual one" (156). But Milkman's response reveals Guitar's moral corruption. Milkman warns him that murder is "a habit. If you do it enough, you can do it to anybody. You know what I mean? A torpedo is a torpedo, I don't care what his reasons. You can off anybody you don't like. You can off me" (162). And Guitar proves him right. He hunts down Milkman and tries to kill him, murdering Pilate by mistake.[20]

Guitar believes that intimacy leads to loss. Milkman believes that intimacy is suicidal. Each of them chooses solitude. And in the Lager the struggle is "of each one against all" (Levi, *Survival in Auschwitz* 38). Milkman is someone who "avoided commitment and strong feelings, and shied away from decisions. He wanted to know as little as possible, to feel only enough to get through the day amiably and to be interesting enough to warrant the curiosity of other people—but not their all-consuming devotion" (181). Milkman desires anonymity above everything else. To be known is to be remarked on; and once remarked on, you become the object of someone's needs, someone's desires. In the Lager "the struggle to survive is without respite, because everyone is desperately and ferociously alone . . . and if someone, by a miracle of savage patience and cunning, finds a new method of avoiding the hardest work, a new art which yields him an ounce of bread, he will try to keep his method secret, and he will be esteemed and respected for this" (Levi, *Survival in Auschwitz* 80). Milkman is full of secrets, full of ways to avoid notice.

Milkman believes that safety only comes when he is "ferociously alone" (80). He wants to be admired without bearing responsibility, wants to be loved without being tied down. Hagar threatens to murder him, so he runs. Yet he admits that he never believed she would kill him. In *The Bluest Eye*, Claudia's total divorce from the community was seen as a positive but in *Song of Solomon* Milkman's decision to elude and escape is shown as an unbearably lonely and morally suspect position, for "while he dreamt of flying, Hagar was dying" (336).

As *Portnoy's Complaint* ends, we find Alex on the doctor's couch, wailing for pity. He cannot go backward, he cannot go forward. For Alex, individualism has become a burden, safety a millstone. Alex wants more. And so does Milkman. Yet their solutions differ. While Alex can imagine intimacy only in sexual terms, Milkman chooses to resurrect his own ethnic history.

Visiting Pilate as a child, he is entranced. He "could have watched her all day: the fingers pulling thread veins from the orange sections, the berry-black lips that made her look as though she wore make-up, the earring" (38). Pilate is the polar opposite of Macon. And she survives because of her belief in community.

There are those who "sharpen one's wits, build up one's patience, strengthen one's willpower" (Levi, *Survival in Auschwitz* 84).[21] There are others who learn "to throttle all dignity and kill all conscience, to climb down into the arena as a beast against other beasts, to let oneself be guided by those unsuspected subterranean forces which sustain families and individuals in cruel times" (84). These are the survivors who, like Macon, misread history. These are the survivors who sink to the oppressor's level, who adapt and become brutal, human proof of social Darwinism. And then there are others who are able to exist "without renunciation of any part of one's own moral world" (84). Pilate is one of those few; she is one of those "superior individuals, made of the stuff of martyrs and saints" (84). "I wish I'd a knowed more people," she says. "I would of loved 'em all" (340).

Pilate represents a tantalizing alternative.[22] She tempts Milkman, but he is afraid to emulate her. Yet, by the end of the novel Milkman recognizes his mistake. You can't just fly off and leave. You can't escape your family. You must find some way of integrating the past into the self and moving on. Pilate must bury her father's bones, must let him rest. And she can do this because Milkman has interpreted the message her father gave her; he has studied history and made it his own.

Pilate is the one person in this book who loves unabashedly. She believes that affection is sustenance. Because she lives out this belief, she is the only character in the book who lives in an untainted world. Milkman needs to believe that "there's got to be at least one more woman like you" (340). Pilate is precious because she has managed what Solomon couldn't manage. She doesn't have to abandon her own family to coast on air. Her wings are always with her, because "without ever leaving the ground, she could fly" (340). Pilate manages to blend survival with an enduring sense of family and, ultimately, community.[23]

While Pilate is courageous, Milkman is motivated by fear. Initially he longs for Hagar, yet when she demands too much, he cuts her loose. Portnoy was unable to allow Mary Jane her humanity. Milkman is similarly brutal. He believes that his survival depends on Hagar's obliteration. "He lay there as still as the morning light, and sucked the world's energy up into his own will. And willed her dead. Either she will kill me or she will drop dead. Either I am to live in this world on my terms or I will die out of it" (129).

Milkman would like to believe that his decision comes out of a western hero's form of bravery, that this is some sort of "high noon" showdown. Yet when she is unable to kill him, his cruel response betrays the fear underlying his resistance: "'If you keep your hands just that way . . . and then bring them down straight, straight and fast, you can drive that knife right smack in your cunt. Why don't you do that? Then all your problems will be over" (130). He cannot feel sympathy, pity, or love for Hagar. He makes her the enemy to justify his disaffection. He wants Hagar gone so that he can maintain his distance, keeping the walls of his safe house intact.

Hagar is no canny survivor, no Mary Jane. Solitude breeds disaster because "she needed what most colored girls needed: a chorus of mamas, grandmamas, aunts, cousins, sisters, neighbors, Sunday school teachers, best girl friends, and what all to give her the strength life demanded of her" (311). Hagar has been brought up to believe that this is the world outside of the Lager, a place where the ethnic community flourishes. Out there "a man is normally not alone, and in his rise or fall is tied to the destinies of his neighbours; so that it is exceptional for anyone to acquire unlimited power, or to fall by a succession of defeats into utter ruin" (Levi, *Survival in Auschwitz* 80). But poor Hagar has been misled. Pilate and Reba are all she has. They are not enough to sustain her.

Hagar's death softens Milkman. He realizes that he never really believed that Hagar "would succeed in killing him, or that she really wanted to. Her weapons, the complete lack of cunning and intelligence, even of conviction, in her attacks were enough to drain away any fear. . . . He had used her—her love, her craziness—and most of all he had used her skulking, bitter vengeance. It made him a star" (304).

Milkman's desire for fame is a canny reflection on the caste stratification in the Lager. He has given in to the desire to become a "prominent," someone who, as Levi notes, is "esteemed and respected" (*Survival* 84). He diminishes Hagar in order to elevate himself. But Milkman realizes that has adopted another familiar pose here, one that he inherited from his father. Macon Dead depends upon superiority; he compares himself with his tenants, with the poorer members of the community, and feels powerful.

Milkman rejects both possibilities; he does not want to continue to maintain a scientist's dispassionate distance, and he feels ashamed of how he has promoted himself. He discovers his kinship with Pilate, who is completely her father's child, born without a navel, without a link to her mother. Pilate and Macon's father was one of Shalimar's children, a child who was lifted up, but was too heavy to be carried off out of slavery. He was the one left behind.

And he was a man who was envied and admired by those who lived nearby. He was "the farmer they wanted to be, the clever irrigator, the peach-tree grower, the hog slaughterer, the wild-turkey roaster, the man who could plow forty in no time flat and sang like an angel" (237). But he was also deceived. This man, this superhuman farmer believed in the possibility of reconstruction, the aptly named moment when blacks were asked to become equal partners in a remade America. Others in his community admire him: "This here is what a man can do if he puts his mind to it and his back to it. . . . We live here. On this planet, in this nation, in this country. . . . Grab this land!" (237). But he is wrong. Macon Dead is shot protecting his dream. His death stands as a lesson.

Marxist critics like Doreatha Drummond Mbalia believe that the concept of individual liberation "leads some Africans to see themselves in isolation from their people, from the community that has in fact shaped, protected, nurtured and guided them" (51).[24] But the only healthy community in this novel is the one Pilate creates. Milkman hopes that there are more women like Pilate out there but the ending of this novel is deliberately ambiguous. He jumps into "the killing arms of his brother" (341). It does "not matter which one of them would give up his ghost" (341).

In *The Bluest Eye* Morrison indicated that a separation from community was the only route to safety. In *Song of Solomon* she shows how separation from the community creates unbearable loneliness and isolation. Yet she cannot imagine a paradisiacal alternative. The moment closest to a resurrection of the golden age happens on the night when Macon Dead stops near his sister's window and peeks inside. There "he felt the irritability of the day drain from him and relished the effortless beauty of the women singing in the candlelight" (30). Pilate's is an ideal "golden age" community founded on love and compassion. Pilate believes that "a human life is precious. You shouldn't fly off and leave it. . . . If you take a life, then you own it" (209). By the end of the novel, Milkman agrees. And when he acknowledges this, he also admits that once he believed himself capable of coldly determining who should live and who should die.

Milkman's world is a world peopled with ghosts, but they have no direct contact with mortals. "You better believe boy, they're here," Freddie, another citizen of the town, tells him (109).[25] In this novel, change comes slowly, almost imperceptibly. When Milkman returns north after his visit to Shalimar, he notes that "there was relief in his mother's crooked smile" (338) and "it was nice. No reconciliation took place between Pilate and Macon . . . and relations between Ruth and Macon were the same and would always be. Just as the consequences of Milkman's own stupidity would remain, and regret would always outweigh the things he was proud of having done" (338-339). His regret is part of what brings change in his family, the opening of a way to tenderness. His regret turns him into a penitent. He has gone from an absence of feeling to a belief in the power of guilt. In *Portnoy's Complaint*, guilt was an unwieldy burden. But in *Song of Solomon* an acknowledgment of guilt is the first step along the road to true salvation. By acknowledging his own complicity, Milkman comes of age. Only now will he be able to search for someone who can share this understanding with him. Yet, although Milkman may imagine a future that contains a means of entrance into some new place where he is not so utterly alone, Morrison is unwilling to show us how he completes this journey.

Guitar becomes one of the Seven Days to take revenge on the whites because "the earth is soggy with black people's blood. And before us Indian blood. Nothing can cure them, and if it keeps on there won't be any of us left and there won't be any land for those who are left" (159). He says, "every one of them is a potential nigger-killer. . . You think Hitler surprised them? You think just because they went to war they thought he was a freak? Hitler's the most natural white man in the world" (156). For Guitar, white men are devils, evil incarnate. But Milkman argues against Guitar's solution. And he is right, in Guitar's hands revenge becomes a dangerous weapon. In *Storyteller*, Leslie Marmon Silko demonized whites. This was a way of reconstructing the Judeo-Christian ladder to power. In *Storyteller* Silko balances her depictions of the brutal white world with her constructed image of the sanctified Indian. But in her most recent novel, *Almanac of the Dead,* all sense of balance is lost. In this novel Silko categorizes whites as devils in order to uphold her futuristic vision; in this new world the oppressors identified with Europeans are paid back in kind, they are exterminated.

Morrison repeatedly focuses on the difficulties of establishing a functioning African-American community in America. And Silko has also examined a dysfunctional Native American community, surrounded and controlled by an oppressive white superstructure. In *Storyteller* (and *Ceremony*) she chose to work from the inside out, fictionalizing life inside of these "double boundaries."[26] However in *Almanac of the Dead,* she focuses on the oppressive white world as much as the Indian world. This novel attempts to define and demystify whiteness.

Silko includes a "Five Hundred Year Map" in her preface to this novel. This is a Faulknerian conceit, Yoknapatawpha county writ large. Faulkner's piece of the south represented a way into his profound examination of southern, indeed confederate, history. He chose to narrow his vision, assuming that his readers would be able to draw the larger parallels. In *Almanac of the Dead*, Silko takes the opposite approach. According to her, this "Almanac of the Dead Five Hundred Year Map foretells the future of all the Americas" (14–15). In the bottom left-hand corner there is a square box with a "Prophecy:" "When Europeans arrived, the Maya, Azteca, Inca cultures had already built great cities and vast networks of roads. Ancient prophecies foretold the arrival of Europeans in the Americas. The Ancient prophecies also foretell the disappearance of all things European" (Preface). The novel itself follows shows the truth of this prophecy. According to Silko, "the Indian Wars have never ended in the Americas. Native Americans acknowledge no borders; they seek nothing less than the return of all tribal lands" (Preface).

Portnoy was unable to find peace in either the new world or the old. Silko's characters are just as alienated. No one, white or Indian, experiences continued familial warmth or communal acceptance. These characters are distrustful, often paranoid. They flail at each other sexually or with murderous intent. Portnoy's howl is alternately amusing, tantalizing, and repulsive, still it is human. Milkman too is remarkably sympathetic. However, Silko denies any real humanity to most of the many characters who people the novel.

Two characters do invoke empathy though. One is the character most intimately identified with Silko's own heritage, a Laguna Indian named Sterling who has been thrown off the Laguna Pueblo reservation. He has been sent away by the tribal council because he took a movie crew to a sacred place, thereby defiling it. Sterling is the ultimate patsy. The council appoints him and "he could not say no" but "the movie crew people seemed only to understand violence and brute force" (90). Sterling is only one man; he has no hope of defeating this invading army. He tries to resign but it is already too late.

Our sympathy lies with Sterling. The council's disapproval, its banishment, is further evidence that Indians cannot nurture their own. However, Sterling's relationship with his aunts is tender. He has returned to the reservation to be with them and nurse them in their old age:"The younger generations of women had not really matched the likes of Aunt Marie and Aunt Nora" (87). Sterling "would think about all the dear old grandaunts now gone on to Cliff House where they had planned a great many of their favorite activities for all eternity. He missed all of them around a table teasing each other, joking about old lovers and sexual escapades" (87). When the tribal council banishes him, his Aunt Marie dies. Sterling believes that "Aunt Marie had calculated her death to shame the Council into reversing its decision" (97). But they refuse to accept the blame, assigning all guilt, all responsibility to Sterling.

Seese is the only other sympathetic character. She is a young white mother who is searching for her lost child. Her baby has been kidnapped by the man who fathered it, a bisexual named David. Seese is a worn-out former druggie; but she, like Sterling, is capable of tenderness. She shows it in her confidences to Sterling, and she shows it when she remembers her child. "After Monte had been kidnapped, Seese could not bear to look at shadows or shapes of clouds, patterns the dampness made on the beach sand, because instantly her brain gave them definite forms. She would see the toy giraffe in a cloud. She would see the print of a small hand left by the splash of a wave" (44).

Unfortunately, these are the only two characters who are allowed moments of tenderness and intimacy. Silko uses them as a framing device for the rest of the business of the novel. Their stories enclose the rest of the massive plot. Yet, despite this decision, she allows their stories no more novelistic weight than the others she investigates. And throughout the rest of the novel, no other character is permitted to indulge in the kind of humanizing moments she gives to Seese and Sterling.

It is impossible to ignore the alliteration here, these two characters' names begin with the same letter as Silko's. I suppose this could be entirely unconscious, yet Silko makes it clear that these two alone are bonded. They are surrounded by a venal mass of humanity. They meet on a ranch owned by Lecha and Zeta, twins who between them hold the secret of the apocalyptic future. The ranch is guarded by attack dogs controlled by Paulie, a man who is described as in love with these animals. "The only time Sterling had ever seen Paulie's face relax and soften was when he was handling the dogs" (38). The dog's names say it all, "Cyanide, Nitroglycerine, Magnum and Stray Bullet" (38). Paulie's intimacy with the dogs is the beginning of Silko's list of white perversions.

*Almanac of the Dead* is a futuristic novel, yet it isn't traditional science fiction. Silko fuses the old stories with her dark vision of the modern world. In order to give the novel a mythic feel, Silko maintains a curious distance from all of her characters. Her voice is dispassionate. She is the scientist, but this time her specialty is forensics. "Albert Fish had been a cannibal and a child molester. He peeled carrots and potatoes to cook with roasts of leg or arm. Mr. Fish had been quite particular about the age and size because they affect flavor and tenderness" (534).

This novel is a novel of revenge. Silko imagines the darkest sort of future in which the disenfranchised will take up arms and overwhelm their oppressors. *Almanac of the Dead* is a long extension of a creation myth which gives Native Americans historical primacy. Not only do Native Americans exist on a time line outside of the banal one invented by Europeans; they existed before Europeans were invented, because "in the beginning / there were no white people in this world / there was nothing European" (*Storyteller* 130). In *Almanac of the Dead*, Silko returns to the final winter when the witchery will have come full circle; during that winter whites will be annihilated.

Silko has a vision of a utopian new world; this world is communal, a world where "it was up to the poorest tribal people and survivors of European genocide to show the remaining humans how all could share and live together on earth, ravished as she was" (749). This idea of a communal future seems a perfect solution to Seese's loneliness and Sterling's isolation. Unfortunately, the bulk of the narrative undercuts this egalitarian rhetoric.

In this novel, if whites are not vicious, they are morally bankrupt and ineffectual. Lecha and Zeta, the twins who hold the key to the cataclysmic future, are half-breeds. Their father is white, but he is without weight in their lives, a moral and worldly failure. He abandons his daughters, then kills himself. His dead body is "as dry and shriveled as a cactus blown down in a drought" (123). This white man doesn't even stink in death, he is that insubstantial. Their mother, a half-white Indian who identifies with whites, dies because she is overtaken by a "jaguar that devoured a live human from the inside out" (116). Their white grandfather is a coward; he won't stop other whites from hanging Indians even though he is married to an Indian woman.

Portnoy is profoundly self-critical, even as he cuts a sexual swath through the WASP world. Milkman disdains the actions of the members of Seven Days, allying himself with Pilate, who would have loved everyone, given the opportunity. Portnoy is sensual; his life is a critical response to discreetly sanitized notions of Jewish sensuality. And Milkman's mother, Ruth, is an illustration of the sad result. Her father's formal attitude has trapped her; her sexuality is expressed in desperate and tellingly perverse ways.

According to Thomas Jefferson, immigrants bring with them a "licentiousness, passing, as is usual, from one extreme to another" (Steinberg 12). Silko's indictment of whiteness imitates this verbal anxiety. She accuses the Europeans and their descendants of sexual misconduct, a desire for the flesh only. In enumerating these sins, she uncovers a personal prejudice, her own homophobia. The one pseudo heroic homosexual character is an ecowarrior who breaks apart the Glen Canyon Dam in a kamikaze mission. His final message reads,

> Dear lover, brothers, mothers and sisters!
> Go out in glory!
> Go out with dignity!
> Go out while you're still feeling good and *looking* good!
> Avenge gay genocide by the U.S. government!
> Die to save the earth (730).

But this suicide note is tainted. Why is this gay male fixated on looking good when he's about to kill himself? If Silko had written a humorous text, we might imagine this as a playful addition. But there isn't a trace of humor in this novel. And this gay activist appears after a voluminous explication of white sexual perversion, perversion that is often homosexual. Indeed, Silko's text is evangelistic, a description of the doomed citizens of Sodom and Gomorrah.

Although there are a host of villains in this novel, gay men are the most morally bankrupt. Seese has had a child with David, a bisexual. He plays Seese off against two male lovers, Eric and Beaufrey. When Eric becomes despondent over this no-win state of affairs and kills himself, David goes to his apartment with a camera to photograph his dead body, laid out in a bloody suicidal pose. This graphic work is his most successful show. Meanwhile Beaufrey has Seese's baby kidnapped. He and David take the baby with them and leave the country. But Beaufrey is vicious and jealous. When he notices that David might actually have some interest in the child, he kidnaps the baby again, then has it killed and sells off its body parts for profit.

Silko's homophobia crosses racial boundary lines. Lecha, one of the twins, has a gay son, Ferro. He has two lovers and "could not believe he had settled for Paulie when something so much finer had been available" (181). Like all the other homosexuals described in the book, Ferro abuses drugs heavily. He has a boyfriend, this is Paulie, the dog lover. And Silko elaborates on bestial perversions. Judge Arne, a man powerful in politics, raises basset hounds. "After martinis, he had sex with the four bitches. His basset stud was a good sport. The bitches were receptive to the dog only twice a year, but they had been trained to accept their master from behind anytime. . . . Nothing was as deliriously potent as the orgasms that seized Arne when he fucked his basset hounds" (657–658).

"White people are unnatural," Guitar tells Milkman (157). Silko would agree. Whites are described as soulless; their income is derived from snuff films and human vivisection. Her modern-day killers are direct descendants of the white colonial invaders. "Hitler got all he knew from the Spanish and Portuguese invaders. De Guzman was the first to make lamp shades out of human skin. . . . De Guzman enjoyed sitting Indian women down on sharp pointed sticks, then piling leather sacks of silver on their laps until the sticks poked right up their guts. In no time the Europeans wiped out millions of Indians" (216).

White sexuality is always perverse. Leah Blue, the wife of a Mafia hit man, has numerous affairs. "She ignored Trigg as she always did when they had sex, and she visualized a brutal French dwarf in a medieval castle who forced her to ride his huge, hairy rod instead" (659). The attention to these sordid fantasies makes one question the reliability of the narrator. Aren't there other ways to delineate someone as morally repugnant? Not for Silko; when she strays from her vision of sexual perversity, she creates the ultimate rejoinder, accusing whites of cannibalism. "There had always been a connection between human cannibals and the aristocracy. Members of European aristocracy were simply more inclined to hunger and crave human flesh and blood because centuries of *le droit du seigneur* had corrupted them absolutely" (535).

The only characters who escape Silko's puritanical wrath are heterosexual nonwhites. Angelita, a Mexican revolutionary, sleeps with El Feo, a resistance leader; and with Bartolomeo, a Cuban agent. In Angelita, this desire for more than one sexual partner is not morally suspect. Her sensuality is "delicious" and "powerful" (522). Calabazas, a Mexican-American smuggler, marries one sister and is in love with another. His betrayal is not malicious or immoral; it is a sad joke. It turns out that his wife is also cheating on him because she is in love with a priest. "How stupid! How blind! How arrogant! A more humble man would have seen it. Sarita had been in love with the monsignor when she had married Calabazas in the cathedral. Her lover had given the Mass and his blessing to their marriage. All of this Calabazas had not seen because he had been in love with Liria. Calabazas had started laughing then" (239).

The revolution in *The Almanac of the Dead* comes from an acknowledgment of common goals. Clinton, an African-American revolutionary, points to "homeless white men and homeless black men" working together "for a common cause—survival" (738). In the end Silko proposes a world where "the streets of downtown Amsterdam were full of Indians from all the tribes of the Americas .... Indians crowding the streets of Amsterdam and no Dutch; many of the Indians had looked pale, as if they had been born there" (756). But there is a problem. It is not with the proposed outcome, a futuristic vision of a merging of races. Rather, it is the path Silko takes to arrive there. Her survival strategy depends on imitation and retaliation.[27] And "this resort to 'identification with the aggressor' is an attempt to share the power by which one feels threatened. For the survivor this means power over death itself" (Lifton 511).

Turning the other cheek may be an unrealistic strategy in a violent world; still, it is redemptive in literature. Portnoy's wail is decidedly more affecting, more human, than any of the complaints registered by the characters in Silko's soulless, disconnected universe. Silko's revolutionaries "must be able to let go of a great many comforts and all things European; but the reward would be peace and harmony with all living things" (710). However, she has not reached that goal. She depends on her European inheritance, the brutal language of oppression and obliteration.

Each of these three novels, *Almanac of the Dead, Song of Solomon,* and *Portnoy's Complaint,* examines the loneliness of the survivor. These survivors have left behind the victims who were "walking ghosts" and "didn't look like people of this world" (Lifton 27). But the dead must be reckoned with. When these writers choose to make the spirit flesh, they are able to invent a world where, for a brief moment lost souls can merge with the living, offering them a philosophy of survival that is heroic and effective

**Notes**

¹"Frequently presented images of a 'golden age,' of 'idyllic childhoods, spent in the bosom of close, harmonious families'. . . this kind of image serves another important function: it is the survivor's effort to reactivate within himself old and profound feelings of love, nurturance and harmony, in order to be able to apply these feelings to his new formulation of life beyond the death immersion" (Lifton 534).

²Both Des Pres and Lifton trust in community as life-sustaining.

³Allen Guttmann suggested that the novel is "like Black Humor—a kind of terminus, a suggestion that the satirist of assimilation has grown tired of the harvest he himself desired" (62), but other critics were more generous. Tony Tanner wrote that *"Portnoy's Complaint* can readily be appreciated and enjoyed by anyone who can recall anything of the awesome mystery and humiliating farce called growing up" (68).

⁴Tanner argues that Portnoy is a "transitonal figure" (68). That seems quite true, though I would disagree with his definition of the word "transitional." Tanner writes that while Portnoy "has left the ghetto he has not yet arrived at a place where he can have a confident new identity" (68). I disagree. I think Portnoy has arrived at a place we are already familiar with simply because Neil perched there in *Goodbye, Columbus.*

⁵Because Roth parallels sexual and political conquest, feminists have had a field day with him. Sarah Blacher Cohen says,"it would seem that Roth's Jewish-American heroes are more immature than the first Hebrew, Abraham. He could respect his women and appreciate their contributions, while Neil Klugman and Alexander Portnoy can only denigrate women and engage in juvenile retaliations against them" (216). But Cohen's feminist analysis of Roth misses the mark in several ways. While it does respond to the cruelty of Portnoy's behavior, it doesn't address who Portnoy is throughout the text. He is a man who tortures himself through self examination.

⁶Stephen Steinberg notes that "the classical expression of the American success legend is found in the hundred or so novels that

Horatio Alger wrote in the late nineteenth century. . . . Alger's unmistakable message was that, whatever the obstacles, the individual can triumph by living an exemplary life and piously observing all the middle-class injunctions concerning hard work and moral rectitude" (83).

[7]Lifton gives this overview of "survivor syndrome": "We recall the guilt-saturated inner sequence of this identity (I almost died; I should have died; I did die, or at least I am not really alive; or if I am alive, it is impure of me to be so; and anything I do which affirms life is also impure and an insult to the dead, who alone are pure)" (504).

[8]See Baumgarten and Gottfried. "What Portnoy does not recognize is that the cause of his neurosis is not just a psychology of guilt but a guilt-inducing politics of fear and anxiety. . . . The paranoia of his parents has a basis in everyday life, as the survivors of this brutal century know full well" (94).

[9]See Shechner for an analysis of Portnoy's inability to accept a middle ground. "Thus Alex Portnoy steers clear of love by laying sexual traps for himself, insuring that his experiments in love with always end in defeat" (126).

[10]In this he is like one of Lifton's portraits of survivors, "the moralist," a man who "over the years . . . engaged in virtually every form of protest" (228). The hibakusha's goal was the banning of nuclear weapons. Portnoy's goal is more in keeping with the work of those elderly Jewish people at a center, whose "survivorhood . . . caused them to intensify their dedication to social justice" (Myerhoff 25).

[11]Sandra Brand, the author of *I Dared to Live,* depends on the same sort of assumptions. She is a Holocaust survivor who carefully plans the murder of a German child. She tells herself that this act of revenge will compensate her for the loss of her own children. Yet when the opportunity arises, she finds that she is helpless. "Unaccountably my fingers had loosened their hold on the gun. I tried to tighten them but the gun slipped from their slack wet grip to the bottom of my pocketbook" (201).

12See Bettelheim's humorous analysis of Roth, "Portnoy Psychoanalyzed." Interestingly enough, Bettelheim offers us little insight into Roth, sticking to a traditional Freudian view. "The father, out of incessant fear for the future, chose and stuck to his job of life insurance salesman. This is internalized by the son as fear for his masculinity" (28). Bettelheim's final analysis is potent: "Is it just another case then of the self-hating Jew living *in exile*?" (34).

13Here, what Lifton describes as "suspicion of counterfeit nurturance" becomes a desire to avoid intimacy.

14Des Pres's analysis of this is critical. He critiques Bettelheim's belief in the adoption of overseer values. "The condition of life-in-death forced a terrible paradox upon survivors. They stayed alive by helping to run the camps, and this fact has led to the belief that prisoners identified not with each other but with their oppressors" (116). He goes on to argue that "the assumption that survivors imitated SS behavior is misleading because it generalizes a limited phenomenon, but also because it overlooks the duality of behavior in extremity" (117).

15 *Portnoy's Complaint* is often analyzed as comedy. See Blair and Hamlin. However, this discounts so much of the larger picture that it ends up diminishing Roth's achievement.

16See Samuels, Hudson, and Weems.

17See Harding and Martin. "In her narratives Morrison rewrites history as a process where present and past interact in a dynamic and always unfinished narrative" (169). Thus any attempt to expunge the past is doomed to failure.

18See Carmean on naming.

19This is a critical misreading of the power of history. She is as naive as the Jews in Nazi Germany who "tried to tell themselves that things couldn't, or wouldn't, get any worse; that the bark of the Nazis, bad as it was, was worse than their bite; that while some other Jews were taken to the camps, they themselves would for some reason or other be saved from such a fate" (Bettelheim 88). Her naivete, like that of the Jewish victims, comes from self-deception and denial.

[20]Cynthia Davis argues that Morrison developed the structure of the text along the lines of the Greek heroic myth. She argues that "Milkman's life follows the pattern of the classic hero, from miraculous birth ... through quest-journey, to final reunion with his double" (16). However, Milkman's life does not simply follow the pattern of quest-journey. Events are responses to an outer reality. Milkman acts responsively, and his response is shaped by the exigencies of an African-American reality. His life is a struggle for survival.

[21]This is the version of self that Bettelheim depended on to sustain himself.

[22] Carmean calls her "a self-delivered and self-sustaining figure of archetypal proportions" (53). Rigney links her to an African archetype, the Great Mother.

[23] Because of this gift, she represents an argument for Des Pres's vision of a survivor who depends on solidarity in extremis.

[24]*The Bluest Eye, Sula,* and *Song of Solomon* all decry the petty jealousies and lack of unity in the African American community.

[25]In *Beloved* these ghosts will offer a key to salvation.

[26]Anya Peterson Royce proposes that many ethnic groups form these double boundaries and that community life takes place inside them. These boundaries consist of "the boundary maintained from within, and the boundary imposed from outside, which results from the process of interaction with others" (29).

[27]Lifton describes this as "an A-bomb for an A-bomb" (79). Silko's strategy is just as obliterating and just as problematic. It depends on what Lifton and Bettelheim defined as identification with the aggressor.

# Chapter Four:
# The Ghost: A Link Between Two Worlds

For Silko, Morrison, and Roth, ghosts are transitional figures. Lifton believes that a survivor strives to reassert a connection with "continuous life," reverting "not only to his personal past but to his historical past as well" (538). In *Ceremony, Beloved,* and *The Ghost Writer* these novelists use a similar literary construct to revitalize the protagonist's connection with a historical past. Ghosts return to bargain with the living. By creating a world where ghosts and mortals walk together, these writers attempt to create a new version of the survivor. This survivor is neither consumed with self nor obsessed with revenge. Roth, Silko, and Morrison present an alternative world where ghosts call their executioners to task, and where acknowledgment of these ghosts can offer a moment of spiritual enlightenment and ethnic celebration.

In *Ceremony* Tayo makes love to the Montano woman, an embodied spirit. "He watched her face, and her eyes never shifted; they were with him while she moved out of her clothes and while she slipped his jeans down his legs, stroking his thighs . . . . He was afraid of being lost, so he repeated trail marks to himself: this is my mouth tasting the salt of her brown breasts; this is my voice calling out to her" (180). Nathan Zuckerman wants to marry Amy Bellette in order to salvage his ruined relationship with family. He knows this will work because Amy is Anne Frank made flesh. And she is a thoroughly modern coed, tantalizingly sensual, a girl from "the country of Fetching" (40). Her escape and her hidden existence leave the power of art "far behind" (155). In *Beloved*, the ghost is a lost daughter who merges with her mother mentally, rather than physically. Though her appeal is not sensual, her appetites are. "I am looking for the join  I am loving my face so much  my dark face so close to me  I want to join  she whispers  she touches me  she knows I want to join  she chews and swallows me  I am gone" (213). Beloved craves intimacy with the mother who has murdered her, but this intimacy is dangerous; Beloved also wants to exact revenge. As she grows stronger, her mother weakens.

According to Silko, the "Europeans did not listen to the souls of their dead. That was the root of all trouble for Europeans" (*Almanac* 604). Allen argues that "while *Ceremony* is ostensibly a tale about a man, Tayo, it is as much and more a tale of two forces: the feminine life force of the universe and the mechanistic death force of the witchery" (*Feminine Landscape* 127). The Montano woman embodies the feminine life force. And in this work, Silko avoids focusing on witchery. Indeed, she avoids describing the white world. Whites have only referential power. Tayo remembers how he and his cousin were accepted by whites after they enlisted: "the first day in Oakland he and Rocky walked down the street together and a big Chrysler stopped in the street and an old white woman rolled down the window and said, 'God bless you, God bless you,' but it was the uniform, not them, she blessed" (41).

In this novel Silko avoids demonizing whites. Perhaps this is because Tayo is half-white. Certainly the situation she invents is unique, and therefore compelling. Tayo is ostracized by the members of his community, but they are Indian and "they are afraid . . . they feel something happening, they can see something happening around them, and it scares them. Indians or Mexicans or whites—most people are afraid of change. They think that if their children have the same color of skin, the same color of eyes, then nothing is changing
. . . They are fools. They blame . . . the ones who look different. That way they don't have to think about what has happened inside themselves" (99–100). In this novel, Silko imagines a new, revitalized world. But this vision is much smaller in scope than the one she offers in *Almanac of the Dead*. Tayo's world is changed inside the borders of the reservation. In this place, Tayo chooses his ethnicity.

The Montano woman serves as Tayo's spiritual guide. She heals him because he has no way of curing himself. Tayo is trapped between two worlds, the world of the living and the world of the dead. But he also stands outside the Indian and white communities. The white world has brought him suffering; the Indian world rejects him. And the Indians who surround him are drowners. They drink too much and complain. Emo, an Indian he has grown up with, says, "You know . . . us Indians deserve something better than this dried-up country round here" (55). Others chime in, pointing out how white society has ignored them.

> "We fought their war for them."
> "Yeah, that's right."
> "Yeah, we did."
> "But they've got *everything*. And we don't get shit, do we? Huh?" (55).

In order to achieve some form of stasis, Tayo must fuse the old ways with the new. His biracial background is critical to his own salvation. His ability to choose Indianness gives him something none of the other characters have, a way of dismissing the lure of white society completely. His rejection depends on the possibility of acceptance that he denies. Indeed, he is the opposite of his cousin Rocky, an Indian who believes he can become white.

The spirit woman is purely Indian, someone Allen defines as "Ts'eh," "the matrix, the creative and life-restoring power" ("Feminine Landscape" 127). Ts'eh claims to be a "Montano," but "Tayo couldn't remember hearing of that family" (223). This imagined and embodied spirit is reminiscent of Silva in the "Yellow Woman" story in *Storyteller*. But in that tale, the embodied spirit took the form of a sexually potent male. In this earlier work, Silko has chosen to create a female spirit. This choice is critical. It reflects a belief in regeneration, a link to the female life force in mother earth. Silko believes that this mother earth has "inestimable power" (*Almanac* 724).

In *Almanac of the Dead* Silko describes the ghost dance as a dance of revenge. The revolutionaries take part in it, and "when they dance, their hearts are reunited with the spirits of beloved ancestors and the loved ones recently lost in the struggle . . . who cry out, who demand justice, and who call the people to take back the Americas" (724). Despite this call for a return to past glory, the reenactment really reflects very little of the original emotional timbre of the ghost dancers. A longing for the "golden age" impelled the original ghost dancers. "The rumor got about: 'The dead are to return. The buffalo are to return. The Dakota people will get back their own way of life. The white people will soon go away, and that will mean happier times for us once more!' That part about the dead returning was what appealed to me. To think I should see my dear mother, grandmother, brothers and sisters again! . . . The people went on and on and could not stop, day or night, hoping perhaps to get a vision of their own dead, or at least to hear of the visions of others. They preferred that to rest or food or sleep. And so I suppose the authorities did think they were crazy—but they weren't. They were only terribly unhappy" (Nabokov 253–255).[1] So ghost dancers were motivated by their sorrow, their sense of loss. By shifting the borders of reality, Silko gives Tayo an opportunity to do what the ghost dancers failed to do. He is able to revitalize and resurrect the "golden age."

When the women of the town finally view Beloved, they acknowledge that this "devil-child is clever . . . and beautiful. It had taken the shape of a pregnant woman, naked and smiling in the heat of the afternoon sun" (261). Beloved's pregnancy has grown while Sethe has been sucked dry. Beloved is no Montano woman. The cure she wants to effect depends on a real proximity to death. She is no generous sexual being. She is a vengeful ghost more in keeping with the raging spirits Silko invokes in *Almanac of the Dead*. Denver, Sethe's daughter, wonders, "What if Beloved really decided to choke her mother?" (104).

Yet Beloved does offer a cure. She has been created to offer a palpable reconciliation with the past. She represents a physical embodiment of the longing for familial and communal acceptance. Before she comes, Denver is lonely to the point of aching, "lonely as a mountain" (104). Denver imagines Beloved as the cure for her solitude. But Beloved's arrival thwarts Sethe's fledgling attempt at erasure. In letting a man into her bed and into her heart, Sethe has attempted to address the "spiritual amputation" that occurs after an event of such magnitude (30).[2] Sethe comes from a place where the old-world views of morality have been perverted.[3] She has attempted protection through assassination and in doing so she has created her own version of morality.

Beloved appears on the day when Paul D, Sethe, and Denver are most like a family, most like what they could have become if Sethe had not taken that vital, defensive step. But Beloved is Sethe's creation. Sethe knows that no future is possible without an acknowledgment of the past. Sethe is a failure. Even when she tries to kill her children, she manages to murder only one. And because of this act, she is never acknowledged as a member of the reborn African-American community. Still Sethe's sacrifice has accomplished something; she and her children are safely out of slavery. Only extreme measures can ensure survival in such a world.

Sethe is a living, breathing reminder of extremity. The community has to reject her, taking comfort only from a denial of her act and the history that provoked it. So Sethe must opt for a new sort of communal life. She chooses to accept Beloved, the revivified embodiment of her homicidal act. With Paul D beside her and "if her boys came back one day, and Denver and Beloved stayed on—well, it would be the way it was supposed to be, no?" (132) But Paul D's fear of the past, his fear of Beloved, provokes disaster, savaging Sethe.

Denver's forgiveness is the salve. She loves and then discards Beloved, admitting her own intimacy with her mother. She sends for the townspeople. Beloved is the impetus for a mending of broken ties. The community unites when it acknowledges her existence. When the townspeople see Beloved, they also see what is universal, the desperation behind Sethe's infanticide.[4]

Amy Bellette, Zuckerman's reenergized version of Anne Frank, is the third ghost in this triad. She is a thoroughly modern woman. When she confronts her mentor, the writer Lonoff, she says, "Oh Manny, would it kill you just to kiss my breasts?" (150).[5] Roth's merging of this modern sensual identity with the identity of the girlish Anne Frank offers Nathan Zuckerman, Roth's protagonist, an unbelievable opportunity. He has finally found the girl of his dreams. She will meet with parental and communal approval. And she will also make love to him. This resuscitation of a world famous survivor in the guise of a fetching coed is an ingenious way of salving Zuckerman's survivor's guilt.

Neil Klugman's distance from family was seen as positive. Alexander Portnoy was torn; as he fled, he idealized the past. In *The Ghost Writer* Nathan Zuckerman's separation from family and community is a worst-case scenario. He is no longer the one doing the rejecting. Instead, he feels "hated and reviled and disowned" (151). This is why Amy could be the perfect bride for Nathan: she acts like a modern girl, capable of sexual intimacy and flagrant desire, yet she is also the ultimate Jewish date.

Zuckerman has been invited to the home of his idol, a famous Jewish writer. Once there, he overhears Lonoff's intimate talk with Amy from the room below. He cannot believe his luck, for in Amy he might find a route to recovery, a road to a future that is both free of guilt and full of sensual promise.

> I kept seeing myself coming back to New Jersey and saying to my family, "I met a marvelous young woman while I was up in New England. I love her and she loves me. We are going to be married."

"Married? But so fast? Nathan, is she Jewish?"
"Yes, she is."
"But who is she?"
"Anne Frank" (195).

Though each of these female spirits has a markedly different personality, they all serve the same purpose. They offer the protagonist a way of bridging the gap between the demands of a problematic ethnic identity and the desire for a sanitized, guilt-free version of self. Silko, Morrison, and Roth imagine a country where ghosts like these exist, to be bargained with, made love to, or finally conquered. In focusing on this particular form of creation, they have drawn up a blueprint for their unique and personal vision of an ethnic American community where their characters could comfortably take up residence.

In *Beloved* the reappearance of the dead daughter is a threat to Sethe, whose passive acceptance of this manifestation of her guilt is her attempt to erase not only the act, but the motivation for it. This denial of history is a continuation of the discourse begun in *The Bluest Eye* when Whitcomb-Church retells the history of colonization and ends with an indictment: "our manhood was defined by acquisitions. Our womanhood by acquiescence" (140). Sethe's acquiescence here threatens to destroy her. Her decline is linked to Beloved's empowerment. Beloved's pregnancy, her actual engorgement of Sethe, is also a metaphor for any attempt to drown out or whitewash history. This denial of the past is what threatened to destroy Milkman. Only in accepting and accommodating his own African-based slave history could Milkman learn how to jump into the arms of his brother, to ride the wind and fly.

Beloved is full of longings, full of emotional depths that must be filled. Beloved believes that, "Sethe's is the face that left me. . . . Her smiling face is the place for me it is the face I lost. . . .She is my face smiling at me" (213). She cannot distinguish her self from her mother's self. She devours her mother, and Sethe permits this engorgement because she is consumed with guilt. She does this because she has bought into the townspeople's version of her story; her act becomes morally impeachable, for what is worse than killing one's own child? She falls prey to guilt because her defense has been one note, full of denial. She explains the murder by saying, "It ain't my job to know what's worse. It's my job to know what is and to keep them away from what I know is terrible. I did that" (165).

This version of history does not reckon with Sethe's survivor's guilt. After the act comes life, Sethe's life. She is faced with the task of incorporation. In order to effect this, she must accept Beloved's continued presence. Beloved is the embodiment of "a past that has not been and cannot be effaced, a moment re-presented to us rather than represented" (Langer 17).

Sethe tells herself that Beloved's appearance is a miracle; and she knows that, as such, it will not stand close examination. When the miracle turns sour, when Beloved enacts revenge instead of salvation, Sethe finds herself too closely bound to disengage. But Sethe is lucky. In this novel Morrison allows the African-American community power to heal. Beloved can be vanquished, the tie between visible and invisible worlds can be broken, only after the town acknowledges her presence. In this novel, Morrison is able to present a rebellious protagonist who finally gains acceptance. Initially, Sethe defies everyone. After the murder, she is surrounded. "Outside a throng, now, of black faces stopped murmuring. Holding the living child, Sethe walked past them in their silence and hers. She climbed into the cart, her profile knife-clean against a cheery blue sky. A profile that shocked them with its clarity. Was her head a bit too high? Her back a little too straight? Probably" (152).

By the end of *Song of Solomon,* Milkman comes to learn to be like his aunt, to love "'em all" (340). As *Beloved* ends, the black community understands and accepts Sethe's reasons for her violent, defensive act. But acceptance alone is not enough. Sethe too must change. And she does. She realizes (just as Milkman does) that if you take a life you owe something back. You can't abandon your dead,'" You just can't fly on off and leave a body'" (*Song of Solomon* 336).

In *The Bluest Eye* the African-American community was destructive, thrusting Pecola out into madness. In that novel, individualism was the only possible route to salvation. In *Beloved* that same community rejects Beloved yet embraces Sethe. "Sethe is running away from her, running, and she feels the emptiness in the hand Sethe has been holding. Now she is running into the faces of the people out there, joining them and leaving Beloved behind" (262). By creating a ghost victim who can be expunged, Morrison offers this community an out. Sethe no longer needs to be ostracized; Beloved has taken her place as an evil totem. And it is not solely Beloved, it is history that is being demonized. When Beloved finds that she has been abandoned, she sees the slavemaster. "They make a hill. A hill of black people, falling. And above them all, rising from his place with a whip in his hand, the man without skin, looking. He is looking at her" (262). The community has forced Beloved back into the shadows. Yet her existence has been noted. Survival depends on more than self here; it depends on the group's acceptance and awareness of complicity, the complicity of those who have attempted to forget. Still, in the end this same African-American community manages to forget "her like a bad dream" for Beloved is "not a story to pass on" (274).

In *Ceremony*, Tayo's residence in the community is as tenuous as Sethe's, but while Sethe has only Beloved to contend with, Tayo has a triad of ghosts. The Montano woman is only the most visible member of this group. Tayo's survivor's guilt has been compounded by the deaths of his cousin and his uncle. His battle at home is indistinguishable from the combat he took part in overseas. "While they fired at the soldiers . . . he watched his uncle fall, and he knew it was Josiah" (8).

Tayo's journey into selfhood requires him to merge with the Montano woman. She has historical and emblematic importance. "He could feel where she had come from, and he understood where she would always be" (*Ceremony* 230). His merging with this woman is markedly different from Sethe's with Beloved, although Beloved and the Montano woman both attempt to educate the object of their affection. In Tayo's case he has to acknowledge this woman's superiority. In return, he gets his cattle back. She is knowledgeable about things that his Indian ancestors knew. "The people had made such traps for a long time because they were easy to build and because they enable one or two people alone to corral many horses or cattle" (210). She is also aware of her own powerful badge of protection. "They won't come down here," she tells him, when he wonders whether he will be pursued (213). The implication is that the place is sacred, special, invisible to whites. And when he asks why they won't come, "she gave him a look that chilled him" (213).[6]

This ghost gives Tayo the ability to discover a way to connect his own personal survival with the survival of his tribe. Now he can live with his Auntie, who "talked to him now the way she had talked to Robert and old Grandma all those years" (259). The Montano woman's sensuality is even more vivid than Amy Gillette's. And Tayo's sexual bond with her gives him the power to transform himself. He arrives at the place Zuckerman angles for, a place where old world acceptance and individuality maintain an uneasy but permanent truce.

It would seem that Amy Bellette could be as complete an answer to communal acceptance as either the Montano woman or Beloved. But Roth denies Zuckerman that satisfaction. He dangles the possibility of salvation in front of him, then leaves him tortured. Zuckerman's response to meeting this apparition made flesh makes this the most farcical of the three ghost stories, and the most full of self. "Oh, marry me, Anne Frank, exonerate me before my outraged elders of this idiotic indictment! Heedless of Jewish feeling? Indifferent to Jewish survival? Brutish about their well-being? Who dares to accuse of such unthinking crimes the husband of Anne Frank!" (210).

Novak argues that Zuckerman "is neither at home in his art nor in the world where his art and his actions are misunderstood" (70). Anne Frank is not only a perfect bride; she is also a perfect mouthpiece. Zuckerman is Amy-Anne; he too would "like at last to be my own. Child Martyr and Holy Saint isn't a position I'm really qualified for anymore. . . . Love has to start somewhere . . . and as for who I am—well . . . you've got to be somebody, don't you." (191).

Tayo and Sethe choose to close a bargain, to find a way of returning to the communities they have been isolated from. Zuckerman toys with this option but realizes that it is only a fantasy. Morrison and Silko offer up female ghosts as ways of purging communal and individual guilt. But Roth finds his survivor's guilt too precious. He rejects the cure. Instead, he continues the act of invention that has begun with this reborn vision of Anne Frank. For Roth believes that survival depends on a continuation of the quest. And his quest is embodied in his art. His tongue-in-cheek description is enough reason to continue. "If only I could have imagined the scene I'd overheard! If only I could invent as presumptuously as real life! If one day I could just *approach* the originality and excitement of what actually goes on!" (151).

Attempts to balance the need for individual survival with the pull of communal and cultural imperatives offer mixed results for these protagonists. The spiritual guides remind both protagonist and audience that they must never be allowed to forget the past. These ghosts are proof that "the pressure of the scream persists" (Des Pres 36).

These writers create characters who can prevail only by defining "a coherent experience of 'I,' a sense of continuity with one's past selves" (Myerhoff 222). In each of these three ghost stories, the author is both literary master and communal scribe. Zuckerman understands that the use of his family life in print is seen as the ultimate betrayal, but he also knows how Jews prize their writers, after all, "storytelling was a passion among these people, absolutely central to their culture" (Myerhoff 37). Zuckerman is a new-world version of the "storyteller." By merging Anne with Amy, Roth creates a world where someone else is allowed to express righteous anger, a world where Zuckerman is freed of his "survivor's guilt."

Amy Bellette is angry, but her anger is justified. She is the ultimate victim, and she "will always be this half-flayed thing" (189). She detests the Nazis because they have taken everything. "I will never be young, I will never be kind or at peace or in love, and I will hate them all my life" (189). By inflating his guilt so that it takes on human form, Zuckerman creates a direct link to the cultural imperatives of the shtetl. In doing so, this Nathan bears more than a passing resemblance to his folktale counterpart "Nathan with a Halo" whose "love . . . gnawed at him like a fatal illness" (Ausubel 65). Yet Zuckerman, unlike his old-world counterpart, chooses to move past his infatuation without integrating the virtues of religious enlightenment. While "in time" the old-world Nathan "became so learned that he sat at the right hand of the master in the House of Study" (Ausubel 168), this new world version has no desire to continue that course of study. He will not be tamed and socialized, subduing his passionate nature. But when he confronts Amy with his version of the story, he finds she cannot offer him a permanent solution. In fact, his well-constructed myth, the ghost he has energized, deflates.

> "It's just that you bear some resemblance to Anne Frank."
> .... "But," she said, bringing her eyes directly up to mine,"I'm afraid I'm not she" (208-209).

However, Nathan's vision of Amy as Anne Frank is more powerful than her thin denial. This is because art is simply more compelling than life. If she is not Anne Frank, he has been witness to the banal outcome of a student-teacher affair. So he and we choose to believe in the more magical alternative. Thus, even after she offers this distracted response, Nathan continues to plan. He wants "to be wed somehow to you, I thought, my unassailable advocate, my invulnerable ally, my shield against their charges of defection and betrayal" (210).

Nathan wishes to create a new world where he will be protected and loved. He wants to be a great writer like Lonoff, because for him "Amy had chosen to become Anne Frank . . . to enchant him, to bewitch him, to break through the scrupulosity and wisdom and the virtue into his imagination and there, as Anne Frank, to become E. I. Lonoff's *femme fatale*" (192). Zuckerman wants to be permitted his sensual nature, his personal achievements, and also somehow salve the guilt he feels. Zuckerman wants to choose to be a Jew, just as Tayo chooses to be Indian. He does not want to be made Jewish "without his free accession, by a hostile society" (*American Jews* 487).

It is convenient for Zuckerman that his relationship with Bellette-Frank will never be possible. She has no interest in Zuckerman, he is invisible to her, as if he, not she, were the vanishing spirit. She desires Lonoff, that "dean of Jewish writers," and Zuckerman can continue his quest alone. By inventing Amy, he has managed to placate those voices from the past, at least momentarily. He has used her as a temporary shield, stilling the accusations of disaffection and communal betrayal. Yet, any real attachment to Amy would mean a commitment to old-style values, and Zuckerman does not want family and home. He wants self, but a self that doesn't constrict, a self that is permitted to reinvent the world and glory in it as his own creation. For as Zuckerman reminds himself, "What *do* I know, other than what I can imagine?" (221).

For Tayo, Sethe, and Nathan, guilt has become a "transformative agent" (Myerhoff 24). Their guilt makes it impossible "to lead the unexamined life" (Myerhoff 24). They are "more afraid of oblivion than pain or death" (Myerhoff 33). To them, oblivion comes if they reject their own ethnic identity. These narratives propose links between historically threatened ethnicity and the individualistic, Americanized survivor.

These protagonists embrace their past, both metaphorically and physically. They do so knowing that "silence, in its primal aspect, is a consequence of terror, of a dissolution of self and world that, once known, can never be fully dispelled" (Des Pres 36). They rage against the silence, to honor the dead. And they bargain with ghosts who were created to prove that the dead can never be dismissed or ignored. These narratives show how "in the survivor's voice the dead's own scream is active" (Des Pres 36).

Tayo goes through ritual acts, through a ceremony of induction, before he is able to acknowledge that "as long as you remember what you have seen, then nothing is gone. As long as you remember, it is part of the story we have together" (231). His ghost and partner points out Tayo's uniqueness. He is someone from two worlds. And after his spiritual reawakening, Tayo "cried the relief he felt at finally seeing the pattern, the way the stories fit together—the old stories, the war stories, their stories—to become the story that was still being told" (246). Tayo's reconnection to his past, his identification with his Indian self, revitalizes him and offers him a way of ratifying his own sanity. He realizes "he had only seen and heard the world as it always was: no boundaries, only transitions through all distances and time" (246). Tayo too has undergone a transition; he has moved from the white world into the Indian world. But this is not the old Indian world that has been obliterated. Rather, it is a new world steeped in the lore of the past. This is a world where knowledge of the old ways comes out of a deliberate choice.

This new world Tayo inhabits is similar to the world Nathan describes when he invests Amy Bellette with Anne Frank's spirit, creating dual citizenship for himself. After all, he imagines himself her husband. Tayo adapts the melting-pot ethic, which depends on the possibility of consensual ethnicity. Instead of spending his life attempting to rid himself of Indianness, a task that is historically and physically impossible, Tayo reverses the positive and negative order. He throws out his white self and celebrates the Indian. When he speaks of the whites, it is clear how completely separate he is: "If the white people never looked beyond the lie, to see that theirs was a nation built on stolen land, then they would never be able to understand how they had been used by the witchery" (*Ceremony* 191). When Tayo becomes wholly Indian, he sees that the destroyers are the true enemy. And these destroyers are the whites who have taken witchery as their own. "The lies devoured white hearts, and for more than two hundred years the white people had worked to fill their emptiness . . . and always they were fooling themselves, and they knew it" (*Ceremony* 191).

Tayo, the half-white, consents and becomes Native American. Werner Sollors would argue that he has attempted to obliterate his "descent."[7] His cousin Rocky attempts an integration with the white world. "The subject was books and scientific knowledge—those things that Rocky had learned to believe in" (*Ceremony* 77). Rocky's belief in the melting pot is familiar. It is an echo of Leon's belief that "we are just as good as them" (*Ceremony* 125). Ultimately the white policeman pursued Leon with vicious, racist abandon. And Chato found that his "fine-sounding English didn't change things" (*Ceremony* 47). In Silko's world any attempt to merge with the destroyers dooms the Indian. Rocky talked "about the places he would live, and the reservation wasn't one of them" but he died in the war, dressed in the white man's uniform. That is all the good his dream of parity brought him (77).

"A fully dressed woman walked out of the water. She barely gained the dry bank of the stream before she sat down and leaned against the mulberry tree" (*Beloved* 50). The invisible becomes visible in these novels; the unsaid is said. Sethe carries the dead with her, and finally it creates the dead, incarnate, which is "Dearly Beloved . . . what she got, settled for was the one word that mattered" (5). When Sethe invokes this ghost of her past, she gets blood and flesh, woman-eating flesh. Sethe attempts to discipline her past, to bury it by unsaying it. But instead, Beloved, her guilt, begins to take her apart piece by piece:

> Denver saw the flesh between her mother's forefinger and thumb fade. Saw Sethe's eyes bright but dead, alert but vacant (242-243).

In order to survive, Sethe must be saved by an outside force. She, like Tayo, is overwhelmed by the conflict between present and past. However, her spiritual rebirth cannot be accomplished through the merging of ghost and human. Because her act was so deadly, it is the visible, physical world that must come to her rescue in no uncertain terms.

The symbiotic relationship of mother and daughter described in *Beloved* has roots in folktales. "This is what one woman did. She was then living in the bush and never showed herself to anyone except her daughter" (Abrahams 314). In both *Beloved* and "Mother Come Back" any integration into society threatens to separate mother from daughter. Furthermore, in *Beloved*, acceptance by society will also sever Sethe from the only power she has been able to adopt as her own, the power to act alone. In the folktale, it is the mother's return to the village, to that closed tribal society, that saves her daughter in the end. The same is true in *Beloved*, for Sethe has two daughters and it is Denver who is saved when the village women arrive. This band of women shoo the ghost daughter away and acknowledge Sethe.

Beloved's appearance has forced the opposite approach to the desire for invisibility. Beloved's development into a fully fleshed out person has forced Sethe outward. Morrison herself makes an argument for "noticing," and it is this kind of noticing that the women of her community must avail themselves of in order to see the ghost. "To notice is to recognize an already discredited difference. To enforce . . . invisibility through silence is to allow the black body a shadowless participation in the dominant cultural body" (*Playing* 10).

In accepting Sethe as its own, the community changes as well. It adopts her defiance. And they, the people of the community, gain from this, for "the first thing they saw was . . . themselves. Younger, stronger, even as little girls lying in the grass asleep. . . . They sat on the porch, ran down to the creek, teased the men, hoisted children on their hips or, if they were the children, straddled the ankles of old men. . . . There they were, young and happy, playing in Baby Sugg's yard, not feeling the envy that surfaced the next day" (258). They receive the blessing of their own past too. By embracing Sethe, they all achieve regeneration.

According to Chief Seattle, "the ashes of our ancestors are sacred and their resting place is hallowed ground" (394). Whites "wander far from the graves of your ancestors and seemingly without regret" (394). Silko predicts doom for whites because of this particular social flaw. The revolution will overtake them because they have ignored their dead and have not listened to the warnings; they have not understood history (*Almanac of the Dead* 604). These three writers are committed to the dead, to the past, even as they imagine a new, more inclusive future. Ghosts are soldiers in the battle between possible and impossible versions of a new world. Sethe, Tayo, and Zuckerman "have done as much fighting as we can with the destroyers and the thieves: as much as we could do and still survive" (*Ceremony* 128). These dead are necessary because they can bear arms, can take up their part in the battle. And these dead can sacrifice themselves yet again for the sake of the living.

Often these ghosts are predatory. And why not? As emblematic victims they have that right. But this feeling of entitlement threatens to swallow these human survivors whole. "When once or twice Sethe tried to assert herself—be the unquestioned mother whose word was law and who knew what was best—Beloved slammed things, wiped the table clean of plates, threw salt on the floor, broke a windowpane" (242). Amy Bellette attempts to break up a marriage and ruin a life. She reports to Lonoff how she "took the sweet name —to impersonate everything that I wasn't" (189). While one of Tayo's ghosts is a spiritual guide, even she scares him. "She must have seen his fear," he reports (213). The other two ghosts in Tayo's life are also vengeful. They cause him to physically sicken. "It was Rocky's smiling face from a long time before, when they were little kids together. He couldn't vomit anymore, and the little face was still there, so he cried at how the world had come undone" (18).

Angry ghosts must be bargained with, then vanquished. Although "remembering seemed unwise," these writers acknowledge that it is their cultural duty to remember (*Beloved* 275). In order to survive, the protagonists must learn to discard their spiritual guides. This is because Morrison, Roth, and Silko believe in George Santayana's most un-American of truths. They know all too well what happens to those who do not study history.

**Notes**

[1]Black Elk's description of his own feelings as a participant echoes this analysis. "I thought of my father and my brother and sister who had left us, and I could not keep the tears from running out of my eyes. I raised my face up to keep them back, but they came out just the same. I cried with my whole heart, and while I cried I thought of my people in despair. I thought of my vision, and how it was promised me that my people should have a place in this earth where they could be happy every day. I thought of them on the wrong road now, but maybe they could be brought back into the hoop again and to the good road" (239).

[2] Langer notes that these attempts are only attempts, the self mended with "artificial limbs" (30). These limbs are "serviceable, efficient, even sources of pleasure and joy. They sustain life, but they do not and cannot replace what has been lopped off" (30).

[3]It is the same universe Langer describes, "this universe of destruction undermined fundamental concepts that normally nurture human consciousness; tragedy, personal destiny, the discipline of private suffering" (28). In the death camps "one survival was usually paid for by someone else's death (and) someone else's execution tainted the life of those who survived" (28).

[4]Accidents of history, as Lifton calls them, for "if Japan or Germany had developed the bomb first, I might have been either among the A-bomb dead or else the American equivalent of a *hibakusha*; just as if my grandparents had not elected to emigrate from Eastern Europe, I might have been a concentration camp victim or survivor" (540).

[5]Lonoff is Roth's version of Malamud.

⁶She is like Silva, that embodiment of mythic Native American power.

⁷Sollors writes, "Descent relations are those defined by anthropologists as relations of 'substance' (by blood or nature): consent relations describe those of 'law' or 'marriage.' Descent language emphasizes our positions as heirs, our hereditary qualities, liabilities, and entitlements; consent language stresses our abilities as mature free agents and 'architects of our fates' to choose our spouses, our destinies and our political systems" (6).

# Chapter Five:
# Afterward

For Silko, Morrison, and Roth, ethnicity is both a privilege and a burden. This uneasiness is familiar to me. I would call myself culturally Jewish. I know little about the tenets of Judaism and have no interest in pursuing a course of study that would enlighten me. However, when faced with anti-Semitic remarks, I become thoroughly Jewish, responding actively and verbally to those who have given affront.

For many years I have taught working-class black and Hispanic students. These students, who have themselves experienced racism, are often eager to stereotype and deride Jews. They are shocked to discover I am Jewish, but they are more shocked when they realize I'm not religious. I consent to be Jewish when the mood strikes. I become, as it were, a defender of the faith. But for me, as for Roth, Judaism goes beyond words like "consent" and "descent," there is something about being a Jew that ghettoizes you permanently. And this has everything to do with Jewish history, a history of exclusion and hatred.

It is quite possible to hide one's Jewishness, to be American on the outside and a Jew internally. And being openly and proudly Jewish does not rule out social inclusion. Jews are white and therefore privileged. Yet many Jews cling to the image of the Jew as a perennial survivor. The Holocaust has tainted our worldview.

In *The Ethnic Myth,* Steinberg wrote that "as a nation we must give up our ethnic heroes and racial villains, and wage a frontal assault against the dangerous divisions of race and class that rend our society" (302). American society is still unable to rise to this challenge. Blacks and whites in America live in sharply defined and culturally different worlds. And whites are still naive when it comes to issues of race.

Lifton wrote of the clannishness of certain ethnic groups, the desire of members to privilege their own experience above the experience of others who come from similarly threatened ethnic backgrounds. It is this kind of privileging that I find most disturbing because ethnic pride can so easily become ethnic cleansing. The war in Bosnia is just one of a host of examples. What is it about ethnicity that is so deceptive and yet so compelling a bond, forcing each of us to identify ourselves as ethnic and as American? This identification does not simply seem to be a desire for political power. It also springs from a basic human desire, a need for family, for a place where one truly belongs. Why else do I automatically identify myself as Jewish as soon as I leave the New York area and search for people with my own physical appearance in what seems to me to be a sea of blond, blue-eyed people with faintly generic faces? I do this out of discomfort and my discomfort with difference is often reworked. I often feel superior.

This book discusses how three writers have tried to address the question of what it means to be an ethnic American. Simple solutions like offering a multicultural agenda, pick one from column A and one from column B, do nothing to address the larger issues. There are basic racial and ethnic inequities. Members of certain ethnic groups must contend with racial and ethnic stereotypes that do more than confound. They make living as an equal member of society simply impossible. This is the case for African Americans and Native Americans. The incipient prejudice is just too great; the indignities of history are too real.

New theories about humanity's inherently warlike, clannish nature have recently been raised by social scientists. When this clannishness makes its way into literature, it turns a writer into a demagogue. In *Almanac of the Dead* Silko gives in to her own righteous anger; she let the worst overtake the best. In becoming like the destroyers, she believes she is enacting her own sort of revenge. But her didactic imperative and her own ethnic privileging undercut the effect. However, when Silko imagines a world where compromise is possible, safety comes from deep-seated emotional yearnings. In *Ceremony* she is able to create a compelling and believable portrait of the survivor. She does it by exposing one precious thing, her protagonist's humanity.

Humanity is not always noble. Portnoy may be amusing, but he is also a whiner. He is selfish and petty, but he is, above all, honest. These writers do not pretend to introduce us to heroic, larger-than-life figures. Their protagonists are everyday heroes. They have flaws of character, flaws of spirit. And these writers do not pretend to have answers. They simply document the daily struggle their protagonists must endure. For a survivor is someone who is canny, who is guilt-ridden, who is hungry for life, and who is, finally, lucky.

Many survival narratives of the 1970s, 1980s, and 1990s are personalized documents detailing an interior journey through depression, or incest, or alcoholism, then reveling in the joy of salvation. One writer who detailed his trip through depression tells us that at the end "my last fears have vanished. . . .I have come to the last words about my season in hell" (Knauth 111). Salvation these days seems to take on the generic tone of a ten-point plan that is good for everyone and makes everyone a sufferer, worthy of being tapped on the head, chosen and saved. Life is much more complicated. And there are no ten-step programs for eradicating racial intolerance. We all harbor prejudice. In class, students often shake their heads when I say this. "We're not racists," they say, and then slowly, or dramatically, depending on my mood, I shake them out of their complacency and prove, invariably, that they are. Each of us has deep-seated fears; and, not surprisingly, many of these have been inculcated through the educational system, little pieces of the American historical puzzle we pay lip service to. Even those of us who are taught to question that staid analysis of virtuous entitlement we call colonial history still bring an unfortunate residue of presumption about privilege.

I suppose that one reason I chose this topic is that I'm disturbed and distressed by misinformation. My students imagine that Jews are in control of this country. The types of comments they make about Jews range from laughable to frightening. Indeed, they echo in exact syntax, the language used by Ford, or should I say his ghostwriter Cameron, in seventy-year-old, anti-Semitic texts. And why should that surprise me? Louis Farrakhan, who sees a worldwide Jewish conspiracy, seems to depend on the same anti-Semitic fairy tales.

Racist language has been employed for the last century and a half in service of a powerful elite who are too often misidentified. And one of the things I've learned in this study is why it is so easy for my students to assume this troubling racial discourse as their own. It has given me a fresh way to respond, to challenge these assumptions and to challenge the language itself. For, after all, I'm not so different. I distrust Germans, all Germans, no matter how many times I tell myself that the Holocaust is long over, that this kind of stereotyping is unfair and, worse, inaccurate. I'm only older and more careful than my students; I hide my beliefs and pretend.

What I might have hoped to find, in examining these three writers, was a neat answer to the troubling questions raised by the assumption of the survivor's pose. What I found instead was that in addressing the pull of their own ethnic persuasions and their own racist feelings, Roth, Morrison, and Silko had no pat solutions to offer. They were simply human. They presented less than perfect worlds in their fiction and offered alternative stances that seemed to indicate a distaste for the oppressor yet mimicked the oppressor's own distaste for them.

These writers are committed to asking and attempting to answer dangerous questions. They are also skillful in creating ways of artfully allowing a character to survive without completely erasing either ethnic identity or American identity. For Roth, for Silko, for Morrison, assimilation is not a virtue; it is a challenge.

# Bibliography

Abrahams, Roger D., ed. *African Folktales*. New York: Pantheon, 1983.

Alba, Richard D. *Ethnic Identity*. New Haven: Yale University Press, 1990.

Allen, Mary. "When She Was Good She Was Horrid." In Harold Bloom, ed., *Philip Roth*. New York: Chelsea House, 1986. 125-148.

Allen, Paula Gunn. "The Feminine Landscape of Leslie Marmon Silko's *Ceremony*. In *Studies in American Indian Literature*. New York: MLA, 1983.

Allen, Paula Gunn. "The Sacred Hoop: A Contemporary Perspective" in *Studies in American Indian Literature*. New York: MLA Publications, 1983.

Arendt, Hannah. *Eichmann in Jerusalem*. New York: Viking, 1970.

Ausubel, Nathan, ed. *A Treasury of Jewish Folklore*. New York: Crown, 1948.

Baumgarten, Murray, and Barbara Gottfried. *Understanding Philip Roth*. Columbia: University of South Carolina Press, 1990.

Bettelheim, Bruno. "Portnoy Psychoanalyzed." In Harold Bloom, ed. *Philip Roth*. New York: Chelsea House, 1986.

Bettelheim, Bruno. *Surviving and Other Essays*. New York: Random House, 1952; Vintage, 1980.

Black Elk. *Black Elk Speaks: Being the Life Story of a Holy Man of the Oglala Sioux*. John G. Neihardt, ed. Lincoln and London: University of Nebraska Press, 1961.

Blair, Walter, and Hamlin Hill. "The Great American Novel." In Sanford Pinsker, ed., *Critical Essays on Phillip Roth*. Boston: Hall, 1982.

Bledsoe, Albert Taylor. "Liberty and Slavery" in E. N. Elliot, ed., *Cotton Is King*. New York: Negro Universities Press, 1969/1860.

Bloom, Harold, ed. *Modern Critical Views: Philip Roth*. New York: Chelsea House, 1986.
Bloom, Harold. *Toni Morrison*. New York: Chelsea House, 1990.
Brand, Sandra. *I Dared to Live*. New York: Shengold Publishers, 1978.
Brown, Dee. *Bury My Heart at Wounded Knee*. New York: Holt, Rinehart and Winston, 1990.
Carmean, Karen. *Toni Morrison's World of Fiction*. Troy, NY: Whitson,1993.
Cartwright, S. A. "Slavery in the Light of Ethnology" in E. N. Elliot, ed., *Cotton Is King*. New York: Negro Universities Press, 1969/1860.
Chief Seattle. "Reply to the U.S. Government." In Lynn Klamkin and Livesey, eds. *Writing about Literature*. New York: Holt, 1986.
Christian, Barbara. *Black Feminist Criticism*. New York: Teachers College, 1985.
Christian, Barbara. *Black Women Novelists*. Westport, CT: Greenwood, 1980.
Cohen, Sarah Blacher. "Philip Roth's Would-Be Patriarchs and their *Shikses* and Shrews." Sanford Pinsker, ed., *Critical Essays on Philip Roth*. Boston: Hall,1982.
Collier, Peter, and David Horowitz. *The Fords: An American Epic*. New York: Simon and Schuster, 1987.
Dearborn, Mary. *Pocahantas's Daughters: Gender and Ethnicity in American Culture*. New York: Oxford University Press, 1987.
Deloria, Vine, Jr. *Custer Died for Your Sins*. New York: Avon, 1969.
Des Pres, Terrence. *The Survivor: An Anatomy of Life in the Death Camps*. New York: Oxford University Press, 1976.
Eisner, Jack. *The Survivor*. New York: Morrow, 1980.
Elliot, E. N., ed., *Cotton Is King and Pro-Slavery Arguments*. New York: Negro Universities Press, 1969.
Ford, Henry. *The International Jew*. Dearborn, MI: Dearborn, 1922.
Gates, Henry Louis, Jr. *Afro-American Literature*. New York : MLA, 1979.
Genovese, Eugene. *Roll Jordan Roll*. New York: Vintage, 1976.
Gerber, David A., ed. *Anti-Semitism in American History*. Chicago and Urbana: University of Illinois Press, 1986.
Gross, Theodore L., ed. *The Literature of American Jews*. New York: Macmillan, 1973.
Halio, Jay L. *Philip Roth Revisited*. New York: Twayne,1992.
Harding, Wendy, and Martin, Jack. *A World of Difference: An Inter-*

*Cultural Study of Toni Morrison's Novels.* Westport, CT: Greenwood, 1994.

Horvitz, Deborah. "Nameless Ghosts: Possession and Dispossession in *Beloved.*" *Studies in American Fiction,* Volume #17, Number 2, Autumn 1989.

Howe, Irving. "Philip Roth Reconsidered," In Sanford Pinsker, ed., *Critical Essays on Philip Roth.* Boston: Hall,1982.

Jahner, Elaine. "A Critical Approach to American Indian Literature." In Paula Gunn Allen ed., *Studies in American Indian Literature.* New York: MLA, 1983. 211-224.

Knauth, Percy. *A Season in Hell.* New York: Harper, 1975.

Kuenz, Jane. "*The Bluest Eye:* Notes on History, Community and Black Female Subjectivity." *African American Review* Number 3.27, 1993. 421-431.

Langer, Lawrence L. *Admitting the Holocaust.* New York: Oxford, 1995.

Lanzmann, Claude. *Shoah.* New York: Pantheon, 1985.

Lasch, Christopher. *The Culture of Narcissism.* New York: Norton, 1978.

Levi, Primo. *The Drowned and the Saved.* New York: Summit, 1986.

Levi, Primo. *Survival in Auschwitz.* Giulio Einaudi, trans. New York: Orion, 1959; Collier, 1961.

Lifton, Robert Jay. *Death in Life: Survivors of Hiroshima.* New York: Random House, 1968; Chapel Hill and London: The University of North Carolina Press, 1991.

Mbalia, Doreatha Drummond. *Toni Morrison's Developing Class Consciousness.* Selinsgrove, PA: Susquehanna University Press; London and Toronto: Associated University Presses, 1991.

McKay, Nellie Y., ed. *Critical Essays on Toni Morrison.* Boston: Hall,1988.

Meister, Richard J., ed. *Race and Ethnicity in Modern America.* New York: Heath, 1974.

Milbauer, Asher, and Donald Watson. *Reading Philip Roth.* New York: St. Martin's, 1988.

Mobley, Marilyn Sanders. *Folk Roots and Mythic Wings in Sarah Orne Jewett and Toni Morrison.* Baton Rouge: Louisiana State University Press, 1991.

Moore, William V. *Indian Wars .* Philadelphia: Gihon, 1850.

Morrison, Toni. *Beloved.* New York: Knopf, 1987.

Morrison, Toni. *The Bluest Eye.* New York: Holt, Rinehart and Winston, 1970; Simon and Schuster, Pocket Books, 1972.

Morrison, Toni. *Playing in the Dark.* Boston: Harvard University Press, 1992.

Morrison,Toni. *Song of Solomon.* New York: Knopf, 1977; New American Library, Signet, 1978.

Morrison,Toni. *Sula.* New York: Knopf, 1973; New American Library, Plume, 1982.

Myerhoff, Barbara. *Number Our Days.* New York: Touchstone, 1978.

Nabakov, Peter. *Native American Testimony.* New York: Viking, 1991.

Nash, Manning. *The Cauldron of Ethnicity in the Modern World.* Chicago: University of Chicago Press, 1989.

Novak, Estelle Gershgoren. "Strangers in a Strange Land: TheHomelessness of Roth's Protagonists." In Asher Z. Milbauer, and Donald G. Watson, eds. *Reading Philip Roth.* New York: St. Martin's, 1988. 50-72.

Parker, Arthur. *Seneca Myths and Folk Tales.* Buffalo, NY: Buffalo Historical Society, 1923; Lincoln and London, Nebraska: University of Nebraska, 1989.

Pinsker, Sanford. *Jewish-American Fiction, 1917–1987.* New York: Twayne, 1992.

Pinsker, Sanford, ed. *Critical Essays on Philip Roth.* Boston: Hall, 1982.

Pollak, Richard. *The Creation of Dr. B.* New York: Simon and Schuster, 1997.

Red Fox, Chief. *The Memoirs of Chief Red Fox.* Greenwich, CT: Fawcett, 1971.

Rigney, Barbara Hill. *The Voices of Toni Morrison.* Columbus: Ohio State University Press, 1991.

Ringer, Benjamin B. and Elinor R. Lawless. *Race, Ethnicity and Society.* New York and London: Routledge, 1989.

Rodgers, Bernard F., Jr. *Philip Roth.* Boston: Hall,1978.

Rosenberg, Ruth. "Seeds in Hard Ground: Black Girlhood in *The Bluest Eye. Black American Literature Forum.* Number 4:21 1987. 435–445.

Roth, Philip. *The Ghost Writer.* New York: Farrar, Straus and Giroux, 1979; Fawcett, 1980.

Roth, Philip. *Goodbye, Columbus and Five Short Stories.* Boston: Houghton Mifflin, 1959; New York: Vintage,1993.

Roth, Philip. *Portnoy's Complaint.* New York: Random House, 1967.

Roth, Philip. "Writing About Jews" in *Reading Myself and Others.* New York: Farrar, Straus and Giroux, 1975.

Royce, Anya Peterson. *Ethnic Identity.* Bloomington: Indiana University Press, 1982.
Samuels, Wilfred D., and Hudson-Weems, Clenora. *Toni Morrison.* New York: Twayne, 1990.
Schechner, Mark. "Philip Roth." In Sanford Pinsker, ed. *Critical Essays on Philip Roth.* Boston: Hall, 1982.
Silko, Leslie Marmon. *Almanac of the Dead.* New York: Simon and Schuster, 1991; Viking Penguin, 1992.
Silko, Leslie Marmon. *Ceremony.* New York: Viking Penguin, 1977,1986.
Silko, Leslie Marmon. *Storyteller.* New York: Little, Brown, 1981.
Silko, Leslie Marmon, and James Wright. *The Delicacy and Strength of Lace.* Saint Paul, MN: Graywolf, 1986.
Sollors, Werner. *Beyond Ethnicity.* New York: Oxford University Press, 1986.
Spiegelman, Art. *Maus.* New York: Pantheon, 1986.
Steinberg, Stephen. *The Ethnic Myth: Race, Ethnicity and Class in America.* New York: Atheneum, 1981.
Stepto, Robert. "Intimate Things in Place: A Conversation with Toni Morrison." In Danille Taylor Guthrie, ed. *Conversations with Toni Morrison.* Jackson: University Press of Mississippi, 1970. 10–29.
Sutton, Nina. *Bettelheim: A Life and Legacy.* New York: Basic, 1996.
Swan, Edith. "Feminine Perspectives at Laguna Pueblo: Silko's *Ceremony.*" *Tulsa Studies in Women's Literature.* Number 2.11, 1992. 309–325.
Tanner, Tony. "*Portnoy's Complaint:* The Settling of Scores! The Pursuit of Dreams!" in *Modern Critical Views of Philip Roth.* New York: Chelsea House, 1986.
Trosper, Ronald L. "American Indian Nationalism and Frontier Expansion" In Charles F. Keyes, ed. *Ethnic Change.* Seattle: University of Washington Press.
Turner, Frederick W., III. *The Portable North American Indian Reader.* New York: Viking, 1974.
Wallace, Anthony F. C. *The Death and Rebirth of the Seneca.* New York: Knopf, 1970.
Waters, Mary C. *Ethnic Options.* Berkeley: University of California Press, 1990.
White, Henry. *Indian Battles.* New York: Evans, 1859.
Wiget, Andrew. "Identity, Voice and Authority: Artist-Audience Relations in Native American Literature."*World Literature Today.* Number 6.2, 1992. 258–261.

Wynne, Barry. *The Man Who Refused to Die.* New York: Dutton, 1966.

# *Studies on Themes and Motifs in Literature*

The series is designed to advance the publication of research pertaining to themes and motifs in literature. The studies cover cross-cultural patterns as well as the entire range of national literatures. They trace the development and use of themes and motifs over extended periods, elucidate the significance of specific themes or motifs for the formation of period styles, and analyze the unique structural function of themes and motifs. By examining themes or motifs in the work of an author or period, the studies point to the impulses authors received from literary tradition, the choices made, and the creative transformation of the cultural heritage. The series will include publications of colloquia and theoretical studies that contribute to a greater understanding of literature.

For additional information about this series or for the submission of manuscripts, please contact:

Peter Lang Publishing
Acquisitions Dept.
516 N. Charles St., 2nd Floor
Baltimore, MD 21201